Day to Day Reflections

Galatians, Ephesians, Philippians, Colossians, Thessalonians, Timothy, Titus, Philemon

Dr. Beverly Turner

CITIOFBOOKS, INC.
3736 Eubank NE Suite A1
Albuquerque, NM 87111-3579
www.citiofbooks.com

Hotline: 1 (877) 389-2759
Fax: 1 (505) 930-7244

Ordering Information:
Quantity sales. Special discounts are available on quantity purchases by corporations, associations, and others. For details, contact the publisher at the address above.

Printed in the United States of America.

ISBN-13:   Softcover   979-8-90124-338-1
                eBook   979-8-90124-340-4
                Hardback   979-8-90124-339-8

Library of Congress Control Number: 2026909768

Dear friend,

We are going to spend the next 376 days reading through Paul's letters to the Christians who reside in Galatia, Ephesus, Phillipi, Colossae, and Thessalonica, and, to his friends, Timothy, Titus and Philemon. While reading through these letters, spend time pondering the messages to the intended recipients, and consider the application of those messages to your life today. Each day has been purposely written in an abbreviated form, for you to spend time with Jesus in your busy schedule. There is also opportunity for you to delve deeper. I pray that you will allow the Holy Spirit to open up the scriptures to you for you to assimilate them into your life, as you are being transformed into the person Jesus wants you to become. May you be thrilled about the truth of God's Word in your life and your world today.

Blessings,

Beverley

Day 1

Paul, an apostle - sent not from men nor by a man, but by Jesus Christ and God the Father, who raised him from the dead - and all the brothers and sisters with me, To the churches in Galatia. Galatians1:1,2

Paul identifies himself as an apostle sent by God to spread the good news. His letter is to the saints in Galacia, it is also a powerful and timely message for us to ponder, digest and assimilate into our lives. See him introduce himself also in 1 Corinthians 1:1, 2 Corinthians 1:1, Ephesians 1:1, Philippians 1:1, etc. Paul's pen was prolific as he wrote, inspired by the Holy Spirit to the Saints in Asia Minor and Rome.

Prayer: Dear Heavenly Father, How great is your story of redemption. Thank you for your willingness to come to this woeful earth to save sinners like me. I love you and am deeply grateful you included me in your redemption plan. I will reach out to others with the wonderful news of the Gospel. Amen

Journal

____

____

____

____

____

Day 2

Grace and peace to you from God our Father and the Lord Jesus Christ....
Galatians 1:3

Paul begins his letter with a blessing of grace - God's unmerited favor; and peace - which is total wellbeing and security that God provides those who are at peace with him.

Interestingly, this greeting is echoed in the conclusion of Paul's letters so that his letters stand framed between the greeting and benediction. Don't you love the way the inspired word of God dovetails like this, and this is not the only example of God's literary master mindedness. Isn't He wonderful and intriguing?

Prayer: Dear Heavenly Father, You are amazing and you astound me continually with your wonderful, thoughtful and truthful ways. Thank you for being in my life. I worship and love you. Amen.

Journal

____

____

____

____

____

Day 3

…who gave himself for our sins to rescue us from the present evil age, according to the will of our God and Father, to whom be glory for ever and ever. Amen. Galatians 1:4,5

2 Corinthians 4:4 tells us that the god of this world has 'blinded the eyes of unbelievers so that they cannot see the light of the gospel of the glory of Christ, which is the image of God.' The Lord Jesus Christ volunteered to give himself to rescue us from the god of this world and the wickedness which is generated through godlessness. He came to show us a better world, and how to live successfully by following his example.

Prayer: Dear Heavenly Father, Your plan of salvation is unfathomable and perfect. I accept. Show me the better way to live so I can be transformed into your likeness. Amen.

Journal

____

____

____

____

Day 4

I am astonished that you are so quickly deserting the one who called you to live in the grace of Christ and are turning to a different gospel - which is really, no gospel at all. Galatians 1:6, 7a

In context, Paul is referring to those Christians who have chosen to follow the Judiazers - a sect who believe the Judiastic rituals must still be followed as a Christian. One example is circumcision. Paul's purpose in writing to the Galatians was to preach 'justification by faith'. We will see his rhetoric as we continue through this study. Thought - it is easy to follow the latest ideological fad, but a wise person would first check its premise with the scriptures. Our world has been and still is full of Christian sects. Be on guard.

Prayer: Dear Heavenly Father, Guard my mind, my heart, my thoughts, my will, my speech and my relationships. I surrender them to you and trust for you to guide me into all truth. Put guardrails in my life so I can hear your still small voice speaking to me. Give me strength and power to hear your voice and obey you, particularly in circumstances when temptation is great. Amen.

Journal

____

____

____

____

____

Day 5

Evidently some people are throwing you into confusion and are trying to pervert the Gospel of Christ. Galatians 1:7b

Here, Paul is referring to the Judiazers who are trying to confuse the gospel into something you have to earn, rather than the gospel being given as a free gift by faith in Him. Even in our days, people are thrown into confusion with popular new ideas which do not align completely with the gospel of Christ. Be on your guard. Keep your beliefs aligned with Biblical truths, and be vigilant to pray, seek the Lord and submit yourself to him.

Prayer: Dear Heavenly Father, I give myself to you as a living sacrifice. Take my heart, my mind, my will, my being and protect them from the wiles of the enemy. I trust in you and I trust in your words. Help me to memorize your word so I can use them as a weapon against the enemy, just as Jesus did. Amen.

Journal

____

____

____

____

____

Day 6

But even if we or an angel from heaven should preach a gospel other than the one, we preached to you, let them be under God's curse! Galatians 1:8

It is a terrible thing to add to or take away words from God's word. See Revelation 22:18,19. God's word is inspired, truthful, enlightening, instructional, rebuking and preparatory. See 1 Timothy 3:16,17

May you keep yourself loving the truths of his word. Read it and assimilate it into your life. It is healing and refreshing.

Prayer: Dear Heavenly Father, I love your pure words, it is a lamp to my feet and a light to my path. Keep my mind and heart on the truth of your word. Keep me in community with other Christians who are walking life with you. Amen.

Journal

____
____
____
____
____

Day 7

As we have already said, so now I say it again: If anyone is preaching to you a gospel other that what you have accepted, let them be under God's curse! Galatians 1:9

Paul reiterates his statement, to be certain his message was clear and emphatic. As we read on, you will see his statements are preparatory for the truth of our Christian faith, that we are saved by faith alone, and not by any deed we have done or will do.

Journal any situation where you felt self-righteous and prayed for the Lord's healing touch in that situation/attitude. Journal God's answer to your prayer.

Prayer: Dear Heavenly Father, Thank you God you are a prayer answering God. You listen to my worship, praise and requests. Your ear is 'pricked up and bending over' so you can hear me better. Thank you for helping me to understand what you are showing me about myself. Give me strength to reach out to you for your healing touch. Amen.

Journal

____

____

____

____

____

Day 8

Am I now trying to win the approval of human beings, or of God? Or am I trying to please people? If I were still trying to please people, I would not be a servant of Christ. Galatians1:10

Before Paul became a Christ follower, he was a devout Pharisee. His leaders and mentors were delighted by his antichristian rhetoric and actions. But, he met Jesus on his way to fulfill a murderous plot against Christians, which was sanctioned and approved by the Pharisees. Hence his statement about being a 'servant of Christ'.

How do you relate to this statement? Journal your thoughts.

Prayer: Dear Heavenly Father, Keep me true to you. There is a 'race' of life to be run, there are victories to be won, give me power, every hour to be true to you. Amen.

Journal

____

____

____

____

____

Day 9

I want you to know, brothers and sisters, that the gospel I preached is not of human origin. I did not receive it from any man, nor was I taught it; rather, I received it by revelation from Jesus Christ. Galatians 1:11,12

Paul is stating where he received the knowledge of the gospel, and who he received it from. His knowledge of the gospel which he preaches was given him from the highest authority, Jesus Christ himself, through revelation.

Today, Journal experiences of revelation you have had from the Lord, what you did with it and the outcomes. Praise God for his gracious love reaching out to you every day.

Prayer: Dear Heavenly Father, Hallelujah and praise you, Lord. Your gracious love reaches out to me every day. Help me to extend that love to those around me, so in turn, they will bow their knees to you. Amen.

Journal

____

____

____

____

____

Day 10

For you have heard of my previous way of life in Judiasm, how intensely I persecuted the Church of God, and tried to destroy it. Galatians 1:13

Paul self discloses aspects if his life, before he met Jesus, to his readers. In essence, he was a man Christians hid from and one of the reasons they went underground.

Are you persecuted for your faith? Who persecuted you and how? Journal your thoughts and feelings about these situations.

Prayer: Dear Heavenly Father, Today I want to pray for those in my life who persecute me because I love you. I pray for *(name your persecutors)* that they may see you in me and be won to you by the love I show them - your love - you told us to love our enemies. Amen

Journal

____

____

____

____

____

Day 11

I was advancing in Judaism beyond many of my own age among my people and was extremely zealous for the traditions of my fathers. Galatians 1:14

The 'traditions of the fathers' Paul refers to were oral traditions which were passed on from one generation to the next generation and so on. Paul's zeal set him apart from others, though, initially it was directed toward Judaism, but God turned it around to become zeal for the Gospel of Jesus Christ.

Prayer: Dear Heavenly Father, create in me a zeal in my commitment to you, to spread the life changing news of the gospel among those I live, work and play. Amen.

Journal

____

____

____

____

Day 12

But when God, who set me apart from my mother's womb and called me by his grace, was pleased to reveal his son to me so that I might preach him among the Gentiles, my immediate response was not to consult any human being. I did not go up to Jerusalem to see those who were apostles before I was, but I went to Arabia. Later returned to Damascus. Galatians 1:15-17

Jerusalem was the city where Christianity was birthed, as it is the city where Jesus died and rose again to new life. It was also the center for Judiasm. Paul is describing to his readers the process of his Christian education - it was through revelation by God and not through the teaching of man. Note: a Gentile is any person who is not Jewish.

Revelation from God is a 'Rhema' or a 'quickened word'. Have you received a 'rhema' from the Lord? Look for them in your life. Journal your rhema's.

Prayer: Dear Heavenly Father, please speak to my heart today. Help me to have listening ears to detect your still small voice as you speak to me. Do not let the busyness of life block out the things you want to tell me. Help me to listen. Amen.

Journal

____

____

____

____

____

Day 13

Then after three years, I went up to Jerusalem to get acquainted with Cephas and stayed with him for fifteen days. I saw none of the other apostles - only James, the Lord's brother. Galatians 1:18,19

Paul continues to give a report regarding his activities following his conversion. No doubt, those three years he spent searching the Old Testament scriptures and found Jesus, the Messiah everywhere. What a blessing he must have felt.

It is a blessing for us as well when we see Jesus in the midst of the questions we have and the answers we are searching for. Journal some of these occasions and spend some time praising Jesus for always being with you.

Prayer: Dear Heavenly Father, Then sings my soul, my Savior God to me, how great you are, how great you are. Then sings my soul, my Savior God to me, how great you are, how great you are. (*sing along*)

Journal

____

____

____

____

____

Day 14

I assure you before God that what I am writing you is no lie. Then I went to Syria and Cilicia. I was personally unknown to the churches in Judea that are in Christ. They only heard the report: 'The man who formerly persecuted us is now preaching the faith he once tried to destroy.' And they praised God because of me. Galatians 1:20-24

This section is a continuation of the last few verses, illustrating the miracle of his conversion. Here Paul discloses his activities again, reporting on his travels and his anonymity.

Journal miracles you have experienced. Praise God for each of them.

Prayer: Dear Heavenly Father, Thank you for the amazing miracles you have performed, are performing, and will perform in my life. (*mention each one, and praise God for them*). Amen.

Journal

____

____

____

____

____

Day 15

Then after fourteen years, I went up again to Jerusalem, this time with Barnabas. I took Titus along also. Galatians 2:1

Barnabas was sent from the church in Jerusalem to minister in Antioch. While there he chose to look for Paul, who was in his home town of Tarsus. Together they ministered in Antioch. See Acts 11:22-26. Paul took him to Jerusalem with him as he was a known and trusted man to the church there. This was fourteen years after Paul's initial visit to the church in Jerusalem. Paul was misjudged by many throughout his life, as we can see already in Galatia. He had to prove his authenticity

Have you ever been misjudged? Journal your experience, pray for those who misjudged you and about the situation. Forgive those involved.

Prayer: Dear Heavenly Father, I forgive *(name the people)* for *(name the event)* as you forgave me. Bless each of them with your love, goodness and grace. Help me to love them with your love too. Amen.

Journal

____

____

____

____

____

Day 16

I went in response to a revelation and meeting privately with those esteemed as leaders, I presented to them the gospel that I preach among the Gentiles. I wanted to be sure I was not running and had not been running my race in vain. Yet not even Titus, who was with me, was compelled to be circumcised, even though he was a Greek. Galatians 2:2,3

Paul went to Jerusalem with his friends, to discuss Christianity and Judiasm with the leaders of the Christian church. There was a conference among the leadership to discuss this matter. This is known as the 'Council at Jerusalem', where it was decided that Gentiles who become Christians do not have to practice the laws of Judiasm, but do need to abstain from food sacrificed to idols, from blood, from meat of strangled animals and from sexual immorality (Acts 15:29). As you will also see in the forthcoming scriptures, justification by faith and not by works, prevailed. This was Martin Luther's stance as well. Interesting how history repeats itself.

Prayer: Dear Heavenly Father, Thank you for your word which teaches, guides, directs, reproves, and instructs us so I can grow to be the person who pleases you. Thank you for your Holy Bible which is full of examples and instruction for me. Amen.

Journal

Day 17

This matter, arose, because some false believers had infiltrated our ranks to spy on the freedom we have in Christ Jesus and to make us slaves. Galatians 2:4

These Judiazers held that Christians should be bound to the laws of Moses and Jesus. They had infiltrated the gentile convert communities. However, the gospel Jesus preached freed his followers of sin and those laws which nobody could keep, and focused on the belief in him, our Savior, rather than the laws and traditions which did not free anyone from the guilt of sin. By putting our trust and faith in Christ Jesus, we have the freedom He gives us. Proverbs 3:5,6: 'Trust in the Lord with all your heart and lean not on your own understanding. In all your ways acknowledge him and he will make your paths straight.'

Prayer: Dear Heavenly Father, Praise you for the freedom I have to live life and worship you without unnecessary rules which could confuse the relationship you offer me with yourself. Amen.

Journal

____

____

____

____

____

Day 18

We did not give in to them for a moment, so that the truth of the Gospel might be preserved for you. As for those who were held in high esteem - whatever they were makes no difference to me; God does not show favoritism - they added nothing to my message. Galatians 2:5,6

Paul's resolve to keep the Gospel pure from Judiastic traditions/ rituals continues to be described in these verses. He was up against some 'big boys' in this pursuit fo truth, and he was smart enough, strong enough to effectively present his rhetoric or argument to the Christian leaders. Praise God for men and women like him who take a stand for what is right.

How can you assimilate into your being, these verses we have been reading?

Prayer: Dear Heavenly Father, I want to grow and be transformed into your likeness. Help me to renew my mind, by thinking, doing, saying and living a life which pleases you. Amen.

Journal

____

____

____

____

____

Day 19

On the contrary, they recognized that I had been entrusted with the task of preaching the Gospel to the uncircumcised, just as Peter had been to the circumcised. For God who was at work in Peter as an apostle to the circumcised, was also at work in me as an apostle to the Gentiles. Galatians 2:7,8

Have you noticed how all-encompassing our God is? God set apart apostles especially for the Jews and especially for the Gentiles. Anyone who is not a Jew is a gentile. God's love and plan of salvation is for everyone - no matter who they are and what they have done or where they were born. Salvation is a free gift offered to everyone!! Praise God and Hallelujah.

Prayer: Dear Heavenly Father, oh how I love you. You gave the life of your Son for payment and forgiveness of my sin, what more could you give? Oh, how I love you.

Journal

Day 20

James, Cephas and John, those esteemed as pillars, gave me and Barnabas the right hand of fellowship when they recognized the grace given to me. They agreed that we should go to the Gentiles, and they to the circumcised. All they asked was that we should continue to remember the poor, the very thing I had been eager to do all along. Galatians 2:9,10

Peter and John were Jesus disciples and James was Jesus' brother who became a disciple after Jesus rose from the dead. They were all leaders in the church at Jerusalem. The 'right hand of fellowship' is an expression of friendship/camaraderie.

Who do you extend the 'right hand of fellowship' to? Who else should you extend it to? Journal your thoughts.

Prayer: Dear Heavenly Father, Help me to be kind, friendly and hospitable to those you put in my life. Prompt me to be reaching out to others when I am not hearing your voice, draw me to those who are in my midst. Amen.

Journal

Day 21

When Cephas came to Antioch, I opposed him to his face, because he stood condemned. For before certain men came from James, he used to eat with the Gentiles. But when they arrived, he began to draw back and separate himself from the Gentiles because he was afraid of those who belonged to the circumcision group. Galatians 2:11,12

The circumcision group were the Judiazers who believed circumcision was necessary for salvation. Paul was not afraid to confront Peter about his fear of those Judiazers.

Are you able to confront those who are clearly wrong and stand up for truth and righteousness? Journal your thoughts and feelings about this matter.

Prayer: Dear Heavenly Father, Keep me strong to stand up for righteousness. Give me a heart to tend to the poor, needy, children and victims, and help me to advocate for them - for what is right concerning them. Amen.

Journal

____
____
____
____
____

Day 22

The other Jews joined him in his hypocrisy, so that by their hypocrisy even Barnabas was led astray. When I saw that they were not acting in line with the truth of the gospel, I said to Cephas in front of them all, 'You are a Jew, yet you live like a Gentile and not like a Jew. How is it, then, that you force Gentiles to follow Jewish customs?' Galatians 2:13,14

Oh my, what conflict!! Paul continues his rhetoric in the next few verses. This argument is leading up to the key verse in Galatians, and key to our Christian faith.

Would you be brave to stand up to a respected leader and oppose their unchristian behavior? A whistleblower does stand up for what is wrong. We have seen a lot of whistleblowers in the church in the late 1900's and 2000's. These are men and women standing up for righteousness and speak up when there is immorality, theft, greed, pride, and so on in church leadership.

Prayer: Dear Heavenly Father, Help me to have courage to do the right thing, when things are going awfully wrong. Give me words, zeal and strength to speak out on your behalf. Amen.

Journal

____

____

____

____

____

Day 23

We who are Jews by birth and not sinful Gentiles know that a person is not justified by the works of the law, but by faith in Jesus Christ. So, we, too, have put our faith in Christ Jesus that we may be justified by faith in Christ and not by works of the law, because by the works of the law no one will be justified. Galatians 2:15,16

Paul is arguing against the use of the Old Testament law of circumcision, that made the observance of the law as its grounds for acceptance by God. In these verses Paul states that is not so, but instead, acceptance from God is through faith in Jesus Christ. He later states that it's 'not by works lest any man should boast.' Ephesians 2:9. Justified means: just-as-if-I'd-never-sinned. These verses were the basis of the Reformation movement which Martin Luther spearheaded as he protested against the Roman Catholic Church - creating the title Protestants. Protestant movements preach this verse as their foundation - Justification is by faith in Jesus Christ. Faith is believing even when there is no tangible evidence. Justification is a gift to you from our Heavenly Father meaning 'just as if I'd never sinned'.

Prayer: Dear Heavenly Father, Praise you for your generous and unconditional love to me. Praise you that salvation is a free gift and I do not have to earn it. Praise you for your perfect ways which protect me as your child. Amen.

Journal

____

____

____

____

____

Day 24

But if, in seeking to be justified in Christ, we Jews find ourselves also among the sinners, doesn't that mean that Christ promotes sin? Absolutely not! Galatians 2:17

See Romans 6:1 'Should we go on sinning so that grace may increase? By no means! We died to sin; how can we live in it any longer?' There are so many verses which discuss this matter - the overall theme being that we die to sin and now live a new life of power and the direction of Jesus Christ's example, through the Holy Spirit. Therefore, people will see we have changed and will want to know what happened. This is a teachable (evangelistic) moment.

Prayer: Dear Heavenly Father, Hallelujah, you are in the business of remodeling me, from a sinner, to, a sinner saved by grace. As part of the remodeling process, you transform me by helping me to renew my mind and live a different lifestyle. Amen.

Journal

____

____

____

____

____

Day 25

If I rebuild what I destroyed, then I really would be a lawbreaker. For through the law, I died to the law, so that I might live for God. Galatians 2:18,19

Paul is stating that in dying to the law frees us from the condemnation of the law, and to, instead, live in the freedom which Christ has provided by his sacrifice for us.

Have you found freedom in Christ? Freedom from fear, from unhealthy habits, from anger, from hate? If you need help, bring it to your loving Lord and lay the issues at his feet for healing.

Prayer: Dear Heavenly Father, I trust you with my fears, unhealthy habits, anger, hate (*state other sins*), knowing that they were nailed to your cross when I accepted you into my life and you freed me from those bondages. I leave them at the cross and walk forward with my hand in yours, freed from those things that burdened me. I want to keep my eyes on you so that I don't fall. Amen.

Journal

Day 26

I have been crucified with Christ and I no longer live, but Christ lives in me. The life I now live in the body I live by faith in the Son of God, who loved me and gave himself for me. Galatians 2:20

Being 'crucified with Christ' means a believer dying to sin. Having died to sin we continue living by faith, knowing that Christ is living in and through us by the Holy Spirit.

How do you see this scripture assimilated and established in your life? Journal your thoughts.

Prayer: Dear Heavenly Father, Thank you for your perfect plan of salvation. Thank you that you knew exactly which sacrifice would free us from sin and you willingly, lovingly went ahead and redeemed us, at such a great cost to you. Jesus, I adore you, lay my life before you, how I love you.

Journal

____

____

____

____

____

Day 27

I do not set aside the grace of God, for if righteousness could be gained through the law, Christ died for nothing. Galatians 2:21

The law represents legalism and bigotry, which doesn't work in God's eyes. Christ came to show God's grace and forgiveness by his willingness to die on the cross. Therefore, by being crucified with Christ, we have died to legalism, bigotry, and a sinful nature. The blood of Christ covers all those infractions from God's eyes, and he sees us as renewed men and women, acceptable to him, because of the blood of Christ. We walk in freedom from sin as we keep our hands in the hand of Jesus and follow him. Praise his wonderful name.

Prayer: Dear Heavenly Father, Lord, you are beautiful, your face is all I seek, and when your eyes are on this child, your grace abounds in me. I adore you. Amen.

Journal

____

____

____

____

____

Day 28

You foolish Galatians! Who has bewitched you? Before your very eyes Jesus Christ was clearly portrayed as crucified. I would like to learn just one thing from you: Did you receive the spirit by the works of the law, or by believing what you heard? Galatians 3:1-3

In context, Paul is calling out the philosophy of the Judiazers and challenging his audience about the basis of their faith. The truth is evident in his challenge.

Does this challenge affect you? Today, pray that our Lord will search your heart, and build your faith in him. Journal your thoughts.

Prayer: Dear Heavenly Father, 'Search me Oh God, and know my heart today. See if there be any wicked way in me.' Psalm 139:23-24. Amen

Journal

____

____

____

____

Day 29

Are you so foolish? After beginning by the means of the Spirit are you now trying to finish by means of the flesh? Have you experienced so much in vain - if it really was in vain? Galatians 3:3,4

Harsh words which were probably necessary for the readers to understand the implications of Judiasm. Again, the Judiazers were preaching a form of Christianity where the followers continued with following the law and follow Jesus. The law was impossible to keep, hence 'a new covenant'. Jesus consistently rebuked the Pharisees about their law-abiding hypocrisy. Jesus came to free us of sin which includes legalism and gave us a life of justice and peace as we live in his Spirit - the Holy Spirit.

Prayer: Dear Heavenly Father, Thank you for the freedom I can live in your Holy Spirit. Thank you for living in me in the form of the Holy Spirit. Keep me pure in your sight. Amen.

Journal

____

____

____

____

____

Day 30

So again, I ask, does God give you his Spirit and work miracles among you by the works of the law, or by your believing what you heard? Galatians 3:5

Great question. How would you respond? The law is man made and it misses the mark. Jesus Christ is God, so he hits the mark and deals with sin perfectly. He died so we do not have to. What is required from us is belief in Jesus Christ as our redeemer…. not the law, and faith that Jesus paid for our sin and we are free. We have freedom from sin through faith in Jesus Christ, not the law. Praise God today for his perfect plan of salvation.

Prayer: Dear Heavenly Father, you are a perfect Heavenly Father, who executed a perfect plan of redemption through Jesus Christ. You are perfect in every way. Praise God from whom all blessings flow; praise him all creatures here below; praise him above, you heavenly hosts; praise Father, Son and Holy Ghost. Amen.

Journal

____

____

____

____

____

Day 31

So also, Abraham believed God, and it was credited to him as righteousness. Understand, then, that those who have faith are children of Abraham. Galatians 3:6,7

These are interesting comments as the children of Abraham are physically the Jewish race. Here Paul is referring that any person who believes in Jesus Christ are Abraham's spiritual children. This includes gentiles, or, you and me. We are part of God's family, the children of God. However, being a child of God includes responsibility and heritage.

Journal your thoughts, feelings and praise regarding your inclusion in God's family.

Prayer: Dear Heavenly Father, there are so many pleasant surprises with you - the free gift of salvation through Jesus Christ, freedom from sin, adoption into your family, a heavenly home for eternity. It only gets better. I am overwhelmed by your goodness to me. Thank you for rescuing me and making me a new person. Amen.

Journal

Day 32

Scripture foresaw that God would justify the Gentiles by faith and announced the gospel in advance to Abraham: 'All nations will be blessed through you.' So those who rely on faith are blessed along with Abraham, the man of faith. Galatians 3:8,9

In Romans 4 and Hebrews 11:8-19, Paul develops the theme of Abraham: the man of faith. These verses continue to qualify the concept that gentiles are included in the promises and blessings of the nation of Israel, as they and we have been born, by faith, of the Spirit into the family of God.

Prayer: Dear Heavenly Father, Abba Father, Daddy Father, how wonderful you are. You had your plan from eternity past, you saw me then, you see me now, you loved me then, you love me now. What can I say, but Hallelujah. Amen

Journal

____

____

____

____

____

Day 33

For all who rely on the works of the law are under a curse, as it is written, 'Cursed is everyone who does not continue to do everything written in the Book of the Law.'

Clearly, no one who relies on the Law is justified before God, because 'the righteous will live by faith'. Galatians 3:10,11

Faith is belief in what you don't see or hear; faith is intangible, which is hard, and that is where trust comes in. See Hebrews 11:1. How would you describe your faith in your life? Journal your thoughts and pray over them.

Prayer: Dear Heavenly Father, Grow faith in me that I may trust you more. I want to not lean on my own understanding, but instead acknowledge you in all my ways, so that you will set my path. Amen.

Journal

____

____

____

____

Day 34

The Law is not based on faith; on the contrary, it says, 'the person who does these things will live by them.' Christ redeemed us from the curse of the law, by becoming a curse for us, for it is written: 'Cursed is everyone who is hung on a pole'. Galatians 3:12,13

The cross was offensive to the Jewish nation - it was the Romans most torturous method of execution, and they used it a lot during their occupation of Israel. Jesus was made a 'curse' for us, so we can be free from the curse of sin, by faith, and we are redeemed when we acknowledge his sacrifice for us. Have you ever stopped to consider how perfect God's plan of salvation is? Today, Journal your love towards the Lord and for his sacrifice for you.

Prayer: Dear Heavenly Father, Jesus paid it all, all to him I owe, sin had left its crimson stain, he washed me white as snow. Thank you, thank you, thank you my God and my Savior. Amen.

Journal

____

____

____

____

____

Day 35

He redeemed us in order that the blessing given to Abraham might come to the Gentiles through Christ Jesus, so that by faith we might receive the promise of the Spirit. Galatians 3:14

Praise God he did not forget your or my existence and made provision for us all to receive his Holy Spirit. We are included in the blessing he gave to Abraham. To I ponder what 'receiving the Holy Spirit' in your life means to you. The Holy Spirit is part of the Godhead and is present on earth with each of us. He is present for those who love him, as well as for those who do not know him. Praise God for his wonderful foresight and perfect plan towards you.

Prayer: Dear Heavenly Father, Praise you for sending your Holy Spirit to this earth, so you can be omniscient (everywhere), all knowing, all powerful, all-encompassing toward me on this earth. I accept your Holy Spirit in my life - Jesus is living in me through you.

Journal

____

____

____

____

____

Day 36

Brothers and sisters, let me take an example from every life. Just as no one can set aside or add to a human covenant that has been duly established, so it is in this case. The promises were spoken to Abraham and to his seed. Scripture does not say 'and to seeds' meaning many people, but 'and to your seed', meaning one person, who is Christ. Galatians 3:15,16

The human covenant Paul refers to is probably a last will and testament. We see here, Paul is identifying Christ, as the promised Messiah, from Abraham's seed. Praise our Heavenly Father for his promises which he keeps and which come to fruition. Make a list of promises you to live by each day as you serve your Lord.

Prayer: Dear Heavenly Father, thank you for the many promises you have given me. Thank you for (*name promises*) which I see you fulfill in my life and in the lives of my loved ones. Amen.

Journal

Day 37

What I mean is this. The Law, introduced 430 years later, does not set aside the covenant previously established by God and thus do away with the promise. For if the inheritance depends on the law, then it no longer depends on the promise, but God in his grace gave it to Abraham through a promise. Galatians 3:17,18

The '430 years' later is calculated in round numbers to include Abraham's lineage to Egypt, and the approximately 400 years in bondage, and exodus thereafter. Therefore, this promise is fulfilled with God's leading his people into the promised land. And later, with the coming of the Messiah, Jesus Christ.

Prayer: Dear Heavenly Father, you are so faithful. Thank you, I can depend on you. Your love, care and promises are never ending, they are new and fresh each day. I can depend on your faithfulness. Amen.

Journal

____

____

____

____

____

Day 38

Why, then, was the law given at all? It was added because of transgressions, until the Seed to whom the promise referred had come. The law was given through angels and entrusted to a mediator. A mediator, however, implies more than one party, but God is one. Galatians 3:19,20

See the promise to Abraham in Genesis 12:2,3 and 15:18-20. Before the exodus, Abraham's promise was the center of God's relationship with his people. After the exodus and on Mt Sinai, God gave Moses the Law, which became an additional element to the promise or covenant. At Sinai, Moses was the mediator between God and Israel. Today, because of the cross, Jesus is the mediator between God and man.

Prayer: Dear Heavenly Father, You are so wise. Jesus came to this earth to live as a God/man. He knows our frame because he has been a man. Who better to be our mediator than one who knows the human plight. Thank you for your wisdom, and your love for us so we have a mediator who understands the human condition. Amen.

Journal

____

____

____

____

____

Day 39

Is the law, therefore, opposed to the promises of God? Absolutely not! For if a law had been passed that could impart life, then righteousness would certainly have come by the law. But the Scripture has locked up everything under the control of sin, so that what was promised, being given through faith in Jesus Christ, might be given to those who believe. Galatians 3:21,22

The law is beneficial since it reveals sin and shows people their need for the salvation. Salvation from sin is the promise. Sin alienates God from man, and man from God. We are 'desperados' without God. But, praise God, Jesus Christ was willing to come to this earth to pay that penalty for sin which God requires.

Prayer: Dear Heavenly Father, Praise you for your perfect plan of redemptive salvation to me and to my fellow mankind. Amen.

Journal

____

____

____

____

____

Day 40

Before the coming of this faith, we were held in custody under the law, locked up until the faith that was to come would be revealed. So, the law was our guardian until Christ came that we might be justified by faith. Now that this faith has come, we are no longer under a guardian. Galatians 3:23-25

Jesus came and proclaimed a 'new covenant' - to love one another. We are known as Jesus' disciples because of the love he has given us. See John 13:34

Prayer: Dear Heavenly Father, Thank you that you are Love. Thank you that I can love you because you first loved me, and you sent your Son to die for me, so I can repent from my evil and sinful ways and become redeemed by the blood of Jesus and his resurrection power. Amen.

Journal

____

____

____

____

____

Day 41

So, in Christ Jesus you are all children of God through faith, for all of you who were baptized into Christ have clothed yourselves with Christ. There is neither Jew or Gentile, slave nor free, nor is there male and female, for you are all one in Christ Jesus. If you belong to Christ, then you are Abraham's seed, and heirs according to the promise. Galatians 3:26-29

My, what powerful words these verses contain. There is no hierarchy of people according to God's kingdom, we are one in the Spirit, upon our acceptance, by faith, of the Son of God, Christ Jesus. In his eyes he loves us all equally. Let these powerful words sink into your being today.

Prayer: Dear Heavenly Father, I praise you for your amazing grace and powerful love to me. Thank you for loving me, dying for me, rising for me, and waiting for me. I adore you. Amen

Journal

____

____

____

____

____

Day 42

What I am saying is that as long as the heir is underage, he is no different from a slave, although he owns the whole estate. The heir is subject to guardians and trustees until the time set by his father. So also, when we were underaged, we were in slavery under the elemental spiritual forces of the world. But when the set time had fully come, God sent his Son, born of a woman, born under the law, to redeem those under the law, that we might receive adoption to sonship. Galatians 4:1-5

Jesus Christ came to redeem humankind into a life of salvation, free from the constraints and bondage of sin. Whew, that is big!!! And, it is free, through grace and faith in the Lord Jesus Christ.

Memorize: 1 John 3:1 - See what great love the Father has lavished on us, that we should be called children of God! And that is what we are!

Journal

____

____

____

____

____

Day 43

Because you are his sons, God sent the Spirit of his Son into our hearts, the spirit who calls out 'Abba Father'. So you are no longer a slave, but God's child, and since you are his child, God made you also as an heir. Galatians 4:6,7

The phrase 'Abba Father' indicates a very close relationship with God, something like 'Daddy Father'. How do you feel knowing that Almighty God desires a very personal relationship with you? One through the redemptive salvation which Christ Jesus performed for you. Journal your thoughts.

Prayer: Dear Heavenly Father, I praise you for your unfailing love which you lavish on me. How can I repay you, other that trust you, follow you, love others, follow the example of Jesus, obey your commands, and grow to be more like you. Amen

Journal

____

____

____

____

____

Day 44

Formerly, when you did not know God, you were slaves to those who by nature are not gods. But now that you know God - or rather are known by God - how is it that you are turning back to those weak and miserable forces? Do you wish to be enslaved by them all over again? Galatians 4:8,9

The Galatians, to whom this letter was written, were once pagans, who worshiped 'things' as gods. Paul is pointing out the seeming relapse of going back to those gods, because of the confusion created by the Judiazers. Have you ever been in the situation of temptation to resume old habits? Journal the situation(s) and outcome(s).

Prayer: Dear Heavenly Father, thank you for rescuing me from my old ways. Thank you for your gentle direction as you have helped me to grow. I want to grow in grace and in the knowledge of you and your ways. Amen

Journal

____

____

____

____

____

Day 45

You are observing special days and months and seasons and years! I fear for you, that somehow, I have wasted my efforts on you. Galatians 4:10-11

Observing the special days, months and years refer to the Judiastic observations of the Sabbath, Day of Atonement etc, as a means of salvation and sanctification. Jewish history tells us that they observed them all to gain merit before men and God, but it didn't work. The sacrifice of Christ Jesus on the cross was and is the only acceptable payment for sin, in God's eyes.

Prayer: Dear Heavenly Father, Thank you for paying my debt on the cross at Calvary, and proving your superior power by rising from the dead with your resurrection power. Amazing and humbling. Thank you that Jesus is the only way to you, there is no confusion, only truth and reality. Amen.

Journal

____

____

____

____

____

Day 46

I plead with your brothers and sisters, become like me, for I became like you. You did me no wrong. As you know it was because of an illness that I first preached the Gospel to you,.... Galatians 4:12,13

Nobody is sure what the nature of Paul's illness might have been, but there has been conjecture over the ages that it could have been eye trouble, malaria or a seizure. Whatever it was, Paul's stopover in Galatia was where he first preached there, thus birthing a new church. It's interesting how an illness or crisis in our lives often brings about a new birth or significant changes into our lives. Think about events which have changed the trajectory of your life. Journal the events and outcome.

Prayer: Dear Heavenly Father, I praise you for (*name the events*) which you have allowed in my life so that I stopped to let you help me to do some self-reflection.

Thank you for being with me during those times, and for teaching me, which has helped me to grow to be more like you. Help me to keep my eyes and ears open to you so I will see and hear you and what you want to show me and tell me. I love you Lord. Amen.

Journal

____

____

____

____

____

Day 47

...and even though my illness was a trial to you, you did not treat me with contempt or scorn. Instead, you welcomed me as if I were an angel of God, as If I were Christ Jesus himself. Where, then, is your blessing of me now? I can testify that, if you could have done so, you would have torn out your eyes and given them to me. Have I now become your enemy by telling you the truth? Galatians 4:14-16

Paul extols the Galatians for their unconditional love and hospitality he received from them. Now, let's divert our thoughts to the gift of hospitality. The Galatians were hospitable to Paul in his need. What does hospitality mean to you? How do you open your home to others? Do others open their home to you? Journal your experiences.

Prayer: Dear Heavenly Father, I want to be hospitable toward others. Show me how, where and when to make the move and ask people to dine with me - at home or at a diner. Show me how to be generous and hospitable to those around me. Amen.

Journal

____

____

____

____

____

Day 48

Those people are zealous to win you over, but for no good. What they want is to alienate you from us so that you may have zeal for them. It is fine to be zealous, provided the purpose is good, and to be so always and not just when I am with you. Galatians 4:18,18

Paul is encouraging the Galatians to choose zeal for Christ Jesus and not the philosophy of the Judiazers - which ties them back up into the knots which they have been freed from. Who are you zealous for in your spiritual journey? Are you free from old habits, fears or whatever? Journal your thoughts and pray over them.

Prayer: Dear Heavenly Father, I give you (*name old habits, fears or whatever*) so you will throw them away in your Sea of Forgetfulness. Help me to be strong to not go fishing them back, but to leave them with you. Thank you for your forgiveness and thank you that the blood of Jesus covers over my sin. Amen.

Journal

Day 49

My dear children, for whom I am again in pains of childbirth until Christ is formed in you, how I wish I could be with you now and change my tone, because I am perplexed about you. Galatians 4:19,20

These verses show the care Paul has for the Galatian church, and his concern that they follow the pure truth of the gospel. It is also his prayer and desire for you - these many centuries later. Ask the Lord to search your heart, and give you the strength to stand for truth, no matter what. The Lord loves you and has a wonderful plan for your life. Praise his wonderful name.

Prayer: Dear Heavenly Father, Search me, God, and know my heart; test me and know my anxious thoughts. See if there is any offensive way in me and lead me in the way everlasting. Psalm 139:23,24. Amen.

Journal

____

____

____

____

____

Day 50

Tell me, you who want to be under the law, are you not aware of what the law says? For it is written that Abraham had two sons, one by the slave woman and the other by the free woman. His son by the slave woman was born according to the flesh, but the son by the free woman was born as a result of a divine promise. Galatians 4:21-23

These verses describe the origins of Ishmael and Isaac. Ishmael becoming the father of the Arab nations and Isaac becoming the father of the Jewish nation. They were at enmity with each other then as stepbrothers, as they are today. Pray for peace in the world, thinking of all the wars and destruction to lives, families in those areas, and the subsequent humanitarian issues which arise.

Prayer: Dear Heavenly Father, Oh Lord, as you know, we live in a fallen world where the prince of the air is trying to destroy us all. I pray for peace in the hearts of men and women, leaders, politicians, or regular people, so there will be a moral standard in our community. May I be one of those standing up for righteousness and be a bearer of peace. Amen.

Journal

____

____

____

____

____

Day 51

These things are being taken figuratively. The women represent two covenants. One covenant is from Mt Sinai and bears children who are to be slaves; this is Hagar. Now Hagar stands for Mt Sinai in Arabia and corresponds with the present city of Jerusalem, because she is in slavery with her children. But the Jerusalem that is above is free, and she is our mother. For it is written, 'Be glad, barren woman, you who never bore a child, shout for joy and cry aloud, you who were never in labor, because more are the children of the desolate woman than of her who has a husband.' Galatians 4:24-27

The old covenant is borne through man's efforts - which is how Ishmael was born and is what Paul is referring to in this case. The Messianic covenant was born through promise, which is how Isaac was born, and again, this is what Paul was talking about.

Prayer: Dear Heavenly Father, Thank you for the promised Messiah who is the Lord Jesus Christ. Thank you that he voluntarily came from heaven to save me from my sin. Thank you that he is part of the Godhead. Thank you for your promise fulfilled in him. Amen.

Journal

____

____

____

____

____

Day 52

Now you, brothers and sisters, like Isaac, are children of promise. At that time the son born according to the flesh, persecuted the son that was born by the power of the Spirit. It is the same now. But what does the scripture say? Get rid of the slave woman and her son, for the slave woman's son will never share the inheritance with the free woman's son. Therefore, brothers and sisters, we are not children of the slave woman, but of the free woman.
Galatians 4:28-31

Paul's recommendation is to remove the Judiazers out of the gathering for their teachings enslave people to the law. The Galatian church, are the children of the promise. We are also the children of the promise. How neat is that!! Bow your knees to your God and worship him.

Prayer: Dear Heavenly Father, I love you Lord and I lift my voice, to worship you, my God. Rejoice, my King, in what you hear, let me be a sweet, sweet sound to your ear. Singing Hallelujah, Hallelujah, Hallelujah to the King. Amen.

Journal

____

____

____

____

____

Day 53

It is for freedom that Christ has set us free. Stand firm, then, and do not let yourselves be burdened again by a yoke of slavery. Galatians 5:1

This scripture has been and still is pertinent throughout all ages, it does not get old. We are free from bondage - from the chains of lying, hate, envy, promiscuity, bad/unhealthy habits, greed and more. Praise God for salvation freely given for us, to accept by faith, Jesus' sacrifice on the cross and his resurrection as redemption for our sins.. Journal situations, habits where Jesus has given you freedom. Praise him today for his freedom in you life.

Prayer: Dear Heavenly Father, I praise and honor you for giving me freedom over the bondage of (*name those things you are free from*). Thank you for your power in my life through the Holy Spirit living in me and guiding me into all truth. Amen.

Journal

____

____

____

____

Day 54

Mark my words! I Paul, tell you that if you let yourselves be circumcised, Christ will be of no value to you at all. Again, I declare to every man who lets himself be circumcised that he is obligated to obey the whole law. You who are trying to be justified by the law have been alienated from Christ; you have fallen away from grace. Galatians 5:2-4

These are very direct words to those who were or are tempted to follow the Judiazers. It is either the law or Christ, not both. History shows us that the Israelites couldn't keep the Law as it was imperfect. Jesus came to atone for everyone by a new way, a new covenant, he abolished the old covenant - the law, by his death and resurrection and gave us the new covenant - to love one another as he has loved us.

Prayer: Dear Heavenly Father, I praise you for your wisdom and foresight. Thank you for a new covenant which is not hard to keep, because I love you and want to obey and please you. Show me people you want me to love on. Amen.

Journal

____

____

____

____

____

Day 55

For through the Spirit, we eagerly await by faith the righteousness for which we hope. For in Christ Jesus neither circumcision nor uncircumcision has any value. The only thing that counts is faith expressing itself through love.
Galatians 5:5,6

Here is the essence of Paul's rhetoric: Faith in Christ Jesus, which expresses itself in the love we have for each other on this planet. This faith comes from experiencing forgiveness through Christ Jesus, and the consequential righteousness and love which grows from our relationship with him. How are you doing?

Prayer: Dear Heavenly Father, Help me to reach out to those around me and love on them with your love. Keep my eyes and ears open to needs of those around me, so I can be your hands and feet to serve them and care about them. Amen.

Journal

____

____

____

____

____

Day 56

You were running a good race. Who cut in on you and kept you from obeying the truth? That kind of persuasion does not come from the one who calls you. A little yeast works through the whole batch of dough. Galatians 5:7-9

When the word 'yeast' in the Bible is used as a symbol, it indicates evil or the corrupting influence of false teaching. And, it is pervasive. Have you ever been in a situation where you sense a teaching may not be quite right? What did you do about it? Journal your experience, prayer and outcome.

Prayer: Dear Heavenly Father, Help me to keep my eyes on you and my hand in yours, so I will not via off the path you are leading me. Give me wisdom and knowledge to keep me in your will. Amen.

Journal

____

____

____

____

____

Day 57

I am confident in the Lord that you will take no other view. The one who is throwing you into confusion, whoever that may be, will have to pay the penalty. Brothers and sisters, if I am still preaching circumcision, why am I still being persecuted? In that case the offense of the cross has been abolished. As for those agitators, I wish they would go the whole way and emasculate themselves! Galatians 5:10-12

The cross was an offense to the Judiazers then as it still is today. For to hang on a cross is cursed. However, Paul taught salvation through the cross of Christ Jesus, our Messiah. Notice Paul's sarcasm in the last statement of verse 12. Honor Jesus today, in all you think, say and do.

Memorize Proverbs 3:5,6 - Trust in the Lord with all your heart and lean not on your own understanding; in all your ways submit to him, and he will make your paths straight.

Journal

____

____

____

____

Day 58

You, my brothers and sisters, were called to be free. But do not use your freedom to indulge the flesh, rather, serve one another humbly in love. For the entire law is fulfilled in keeping this one command, 'Love your neighbor as yourself'. If you bite and devour each other, watch out or you will be destroyed by each other. Galatians 5:13-15

Jesus taught 'Kingdom living'. Kingdom living is loving one another, living in the Spirit in a righteous and believing manner, caring for each other here and now. Oh to be rid of those selfish conflicts!!

Prayer: Dear Heavenly Father, Please guard my attitude, speech, thoughts and will. Help me to think before I speak and be slow to anger. Grow your fruit in my life. Amen

Journal

____

____

____

____

____

Day 59

So I say, walk by the Spirit and you will not gratify the desires of the flesh. For the flesh desires what is contrary to the Spirit, and the Spirit what is contrary to the flesh. They are in conflict with each other, so that you are not to do whatever you want. But if you are led by the Spirit you are not under the law. Galatians 5:16-18

In the next few verses, we will see the fruit of a life of the sinful nature, and also the fruit of a life by living in the Spirit. When Jesus comes into our life, he comes as his Holy Spirit, so Paul is urging us to open all the nooks and crannies of our life to Jesus - and his freedom. The fruit of the Spirit will result. Isn't Jesus wonderful?

Prayer: Dear Heavenly Father, I love you, I love your ways, and I love the fruit you grow in me. Help me to be strong to let go of my old ways and let you develop your ways in me. Amen.

Journal

Day 60

The acts of the flesh are obvious: sexual immorality; impurity and debauchery; idolatry and witchcraft; hatred, discord, jealousy, fits of rage, selfish ambition, dissensions, factions and envy; drunkenness, orgies and the like. I warn you, as I did before, that those who live like this will not inherit the kingdom of God. Galatians 5:19-21

Such an ugly list, but some of those are insidious and could easily enter into one's life if the life is unchecked by the Holy Spirit. Also see Romans 1:29-31. Ask the Lord to search your heart today to be aware of any acts of a sinful nature, and ask him forgiveness and strength to overcome.

Prayer: Dear Heavenly Father, I trust you to take care of me. Help me hear your voice when I have become selfish and wayward. Lead me to your path of righteousness. Amen.

Journal

____

____

____

____

____

Day 61

But the Fruit of the Spirit is love, joy, peace, forbearance, kindness, goodness, faithfulness, gentleness and self-control. Against such things there is no law. Galatians 5:22,23

Praise God for hope, and his goodness in providing these lovely 'fruit' generated from a life lived in his presence. Let's look at each of these fruit over the next few days.

Love - this is a genuine brotherly love from the heart - agape love, not to be confused with romantic or erotic love. The new commandment Jesus gave to us is to 'love your neighbor as yourself'. Matthew 19:19. How does this look in your life?

Journal your thoughts and dreams.

Prayer: Dear Heavenly Father, You gave me a new commandment, to love one another as you have love me. I want to love those around me. I want to love my neighbor as myself. Please show me what that looks like and give me the courage and strength to love them in such a way. Amen.

Journal

____

____

____

____

____

Day 62

But the Fruit of the Spirit is love, joy peace, forbearance, kindness, faithfulness, gentleness and self-control. Against such things there is no law.
Galatians 5:22,23

Note: the following definitions are guided by the Oxford Dictionary.

Joy - a gladness welling up from the heart often seen as a happy expression on the face, but also evident by pleasant and caring actions.

Peace - Can be civil or global, but this verse refers to inner peace. An attitude of calmness, quietness with harmonious relationships.

Forebearance/Patience - calmness, particularly in relationships. Indicates care and love with no resentment.

Prayer: Dear Heavenly Father, I'll have each of those. I want to grow them in my life. Teach me your ways and lead me into your truth. Give me courage to open myself up to you and let go of the ugly 'stuff' that holds me back from allowing you to grow your fruit within me. Thank you for your love to me. Amen.

Journal

___

Day 63

But the Fruit of the Spirit is love, joy, peace, forbearance, kindness, faithfulness, gentleness and self-control. Against such things there is no law.
Galatians 5:22,23

Kindness - gentle, benevolent, friendly and considerate.

Faithfulness - Loyalty, true, consistent belief with trust.

Gentleness - freedom from violence, kindly, thoughtful, not rough or severe.

Self-Control - completely able to manage one's emotions, feelings, thoughts and actions in accordance to one's belief. See 2 Timothy 1:7

Prayer: Dear Heavenly Father, I want all of those fruit as well. I give myself to you as a living sacrifice, so you will remove all the ugly 'stuff' and renew me with your Holy Spirit and cleanse me from all the unrighteousness that is within me. Thank you for your care and love to me. Amen.

Journal

____

____

____

____

Day 64

Those who belong to Christ Jesus have crucified the flesh with its passions and desires. Since we live by the Spirit, let us keep in step with the Spirit. Let us not become conceited, provoking and envying each other. Galatians 5:24-26

A reminder that our old sinful nature was crucified with Christ and is now dead.

We walk free of the bondage of sins, by the power of Jesus through the Holy Spirit. How are you doing in your freedom from sin?

Prayer: Dear Heavenly Father, I ask for strength and courage to walk my daily life in the power of the Holy Spirit. Amen.

Journal

____

____

____

____

____

Day 65

Brothers and sisters, if someone is caught in a sin, you who live by the Spirit should restore that person gently. But watch yourself, or you also may be tempted. Galatians 6:1

The Greek word for 'restore' means 'mending nets.' Interesting the connotation here as often mending nets is done together. The word which qualifies 'restore' is 'gently', not harshly or judgmentally!! People respond to guidance when it is provided in an acceptable manner.

Have you experienced or given guidance to another person? What manner did you give it? How did the person respond? How else could it have been done? Journal your thoughts.

Prayer: Dear Heavenly Father, I ask that you empower me with the fruit of gentleness in my life. Grow it to full fruition. Amen

Journal

____

____

____

____

____

Day 66

Carry each others burdens, and in this way you will fulfill the law of Christ.
Galatians 6:2

Jesus gave us a new commandment - see John 13:34, to 'love one another as I (Jesus) have loved you'. This is agape (brotherly) love for each other. To care about each other, our communities, our country's governments (both federal and civil), to care for the poor, widows and orphans. Carrying each other's burdens means to support each other in our weaknesses as well as our strengths.

Who do you care for? Who cares for you? Journal your thoughts.

Prayer: Dear Heavenly Father, I pray for those I care for (*name those whom you care for*), and ask you give me the strength and foresight to help them as you lead me to tend and love on them. Amen

Journal

____

____

____

____

____

Day 67

If anyone thinks they are something when they are not, they deceive themselves. Each one should test their own actions. Then they can take pride in themselves alone, without comparing themselves to somebody else, for each one should carry their own load. Galatians 6:3-5

Each of us is responsible before God. We cannot hide anything from God, he knows anyway, but He wants us recognize sins ourselves, and to confess them to him. Ask God to search your heart and if anything surfaces lay it on the altar before him. Journal your thoughts and actions. Praise God for his love and faithfulness to you.

Prayer: Dear Heavenly Father, Search my heart and show me the things I am not aware of which are not pleasing to you. Give me ears to hear you. Amen.

Journal

____

____

____

____

____

Day 68

Nevertheless, the one who receives instruction in the word should share all good things with their instructor. Do not be deceived, God cannot be mocked. A man reaps what he sows. Galatians 6:6,7

Our job as Christians is to share the good news, it is the multiplication effect. The 'Reaping what you sow' principle refers to both positive or negative sowing and reaping.

Today, take an honest look at your attitudes and actions. Lay them before the Lord and ask for guidance to fix what needs fixing and, praise him for his faithfulness in guiding you.

Prayer: Dear Heavenly Father, Continue searching of my heart. I lay before you (*state your attitudes or actions*) and ask for you to walk with me as I surrender them to you and choose to let you grow me in ways to please you. Keep me strong in my faith. Amen.

Journal

____

____

____

____

____

Day 69

Whoever sows to please their flesh, from the flesh will reap destruction; whoever sows to please the Spirit, from the Spirit will reap eternal life. Galatians 6:8

Again, poignant words to help us to check our attitudes. Interestingly enough, our attitudes are a product of choice - we choose to please the sinful nature, or, we choose to please the Holy Spirit. It's about our will.

What do you choose today? Continue with your soul search, being honest with the Lord. He knows anyway so you don't need to hide anything, but, He wants to hear it from you.

Prayer: Dear Heavenly Father, I praise you for your faithfulness toward me, helping me to be honest before you. Amen.

Journal

____

____

____

____

____

Day 70

Let us not become weary in doing good, for at the proper time we will reap a harvest if we do not give up. Therefore, as we have opportunity, let us do good to all people, especially to those who belong to the family of believers.
Galatians 6:9,10

I hope these verses are an encouragement to you, to continue the good work of kindness and generosity toward your fellow man. People may not see, or recognize your efforts, but God does and he knows.

Thank the Lord for the opportunities he gives you to serve him.

Prayer: Thank you for opportunities you give me to serve him. (*name each of those opportunities*)

Journal

____

____

____

____

Day 71

See what large letters I use as I write to you with my own hand! Those who want to impress by means of the flesh are trying to compel you to be circumcised. The only reason they do this is to avoid being persecuted for the Cross of Christ. Galatians 6:11,12

By advocating circumcision, the Jewish christians were thinking only of themselves. Because, to teach circumcision gave them a lesser degree of persecution from the Jewish opponents to christianity. Isn't sin and deception sickening? Here were a group of people teaching falsehoods to make it easier for themselves to live. This still happens today. The news often reports of the downfall of Christian leaders and their followers because of the sin of following something that pleases themselves and makes life easier for them.

Pray for courage to stand up for the truth. Journal your thoughts.

Prayer: Dear Heavenly Father, I ask for courage to stand up for truth. Give me strength to choose right living (righteousness), rather than ignore injustices and sin around me. Thank you. Amen

Journal

____

____

____

____

____

Day 72

Not even those who are circumcised keep the law, yet they want you to be circumcised, that they may boast about your circumcision in the flesh. May I never boast except in the cross of our Lord Jesus Christ, through which the world has been crucified to me and I to the world. Galatians 6:13,14

The irony of it all!! The Judiazers themselves, couldn't keep the law, but they were teaching the new gentile converts that they should keep the law. Oh, that we keep our lives true, absent of falsehood, so that we will not lead those who watch us, astray.

Journal your thoughts, actions and prayer.

Prayer: Dear Heavenly Father, I don't want to be called a hypocrite in my walk with you. Keep me true to you and my faith in you. Give me ears to hear you and eyes to see those around me who need you. Amen

Journal

____

____

____

____

Day 73

Neither circumcision or uncircumcision means anything, what counts is a new creation. Peace and mercy to all who follow this rule - to the Israel of God. Galatians 6:15,16

Wham!! Paul nailed it! God is looking for new creations who have found freedom and transformation in Christ Jesus. Gone are the 'chains' that bound them and gone is the bondage of old laws which nobody could keep.

At this point do some self-reflection. What are (*if any*) the 'bonds/chains' which bind or bound you, and what is the freedom you now live in through Christ Jesus. Journal your reflections.

Prayer: Dear Heavenly Father, Todayt I bow my knees and raise my hands to praise you. Praise you for your unconditional love and mercy which you lavish upon me. Amen.

Journal

____

____

____

____

____

Day 74

From now on, let no one cause me trouble, for I bear on my body the marks of Jesus. The grace of our Lord Jesus Christ be with your spirit, brothers and sisters. Amen. Galatians 6:17,18

The 'marks of Jesus' statement is probably referring to the stoning and beatings Paul had received, see Acts 14:19, 16:22. Paul always finishes his letters with an encouraging benediction to his letters, as of a father to a son.

How do you leave your loved ones when it is time to leave them? What encouragements do you give them? Journal your thoughts.

Prayer: Dear Heavenly Father, I appreciate those whom you have put next to me in my family, workspace/study space, my leisure and my church. Help me to see them and love on them in your name. Amen.

Journal

____

____

____

____

____

Day 75

Paul, an apostle of Christ Jesus by the will of God. To God's holy people in Ephesus, the faithful in Christ Jesus: Grace and peace to you from God our Father and the Lord Jesus Christ. Ephesians 1:1,2

These verses are Paul's greetings to the church in Ephesus. Did you notice in the first verse he states he is an apostle 'by the will of God'? Paul was not a disciple of Christ Jesus during Jesus' earthly life and was not with Christ Jesus in the upper room. However, he did meet Christ Jesus later, after the ascension, and while Paul was on a murderous trip to kill christians in Damascus - see Acts 1.

Prayer: Dear Heavenly Father, you are amazing, you take us at our worst, and you transform us into your image. It is all because you love us and you have given us the free gift of salvation, so we can receive your forgiveness and become transformed into your image. Wow. Thank you so much. Amen.

Journal

____

____

____

____

____

Day 76

Praise be to God and the Father of our Lord Jesus Christ, who has blessed us in heavenly realms with every spiritual blessing in Christ. For he chose us in him before the creation of the world to be holy and blameless in his sight. Ephesians 1:3-4b

Divine election is a common theme in Paul's letters.... he chose us, he predestined us. Wow, our God is an awesome God. He knows everything from the beginning to the end, and everything in between. And he chose to include us in his plans and purposes, that is why you are here.

Today, prayerfully surrender yourself to him, your time, skill, plans, thoughts, assets and your income.

Prayer: Dear Heavenly Father, I surrender myself to you. I surrender my time, my plans, my assets and my income to you, for your use, as you give to others through me. Thank you for your all-knowing power. Amen.

Journal

____

____

____

____

____

Day 77

In love he predestined us for adoption to sonship through Jesus Christ, in accordance with his pleasure and will - to the praise of his glorious grace, which he has freely given to us in the One he loves. Ephesians 1:4b-6

When the Bible mentions 'sons' it generally means 'sons and daughters'. We have been predestined to be adopted into God's family. God didn't have to adopt us, but he chose to for his pleasure. This occurs because of his love for his son, Christ Jesus and for his love towards you. Our love for and belief in Christ Jesus opens the adoption. How great is that!!!

Prayer: Dear Heavenly Father, Abba Father, Daddy Father. Thank you for welcoming me into your family by adoption, through the acceptance of the sacrifice of Jesus Christ and his resurrection power. Thank you for choosing me. Amen.

Journal

____

____

____

____

Day 78

In him we have redemption through his blood, the forgiveness of sins in accordance with the riches of God's grace, that he lavished on us. With all wisdom and understanding... Ephesians 1:7,8

In Paul's day, the Ephesians were familiar with practice of redemption. It meant that a ransom was paid and slaves were freed. Paul uses the analogy here stating that it was and is necessary to free sinners, us, from the bondage of sin, so Jesus Christ paid the ransom for our freedom.

How do you feel about God lavishing his riches and grace on you? Journal your thoughts.

Prayer: Dear Heavenly Father, You lavish your love on me and I don't deserve it, but I humbly accept all you have done for me. Thank you for redeeming me into your family, that I can live with you for eternity. Amen.

Journal

____

____

____

____

____

Day 79

... he made known to us the mystery of his will according to his good pleasure, which he purposed in Christ, to be put into effect when the times reach their fulfillment - to bring unity to all things in heaven and on earth under Christ. Ephesians 1:9-10

In a world of confusion and turmoil, Jesus Christ came to this earth to set things right. The problem = sin. Jesus Christ came to cancel sin and to offer us a new way of life. Which brings unity to all things in heaven and on the earth under the leadership of the King himself, Jesus Christ, our savior.

Thank you Jesus.

Prayer: Dear Heavenly Father, I acknowledge that you are in control - you have the final say, as we see in the book of Revelation. I submit myself to you, so I can hear your guidance in my life, and see those around me who need to hear about your goodness. Amen.

Journal

____

____

____

____

____

Day 80

In him we were also chosen, having been predestined according to the plan of him who works out everything in conformity with the purpose of his will,... Ephesians 1:8-11

In God's plan of creation and redemption, Christ is the center of everything. Everything focuses on him. He chose us, it is our choice to choose him back. Preplanned is another word for predestined. Know that God almighty planned for a place for you in his kingdom.

Prayer: Dear Heavenly Father, I raise my hands and my heart to praise you for all that you have done - for me and for sinful humans. Amen and Amen

Journal

____

____

____

____

____

Day 81

...in order that we, who were the first to put our hope in Christ, might be for the praise of his glory. And you also were included in Christ when you heard the message of truth, the gospel of your salvation. Ephesians 8:12,13a

Continuing on from yesterday's verses, Paul encourages the Ephesian church reminding them they were some of the first gentile believers for the praise of God, as well as reiterating their security in Christ Jesus.

Do you feel secure in Christ Jesus? Stand on and rest in his promises to you today. Journal promises to stand on and rest in during your day.

Prayer: Dear Heavenly Father, Thank you for your promises to me. I thank you for (*state the promises that have been fulfilled, and those which you have faith for their fulfillment*). Amen

Journal

____

____

____

____

____

Day 82

When you believed, you were marked in him with a seal, the promised Holy Spirit, who is a deposit guaranteeing our inheritance until the redemption of those who are God's possession - to the praise of his glory. Ephesians 1:13b-14

God has not and will not forget you, you are 'marked with a seal' for him. His Holy Spirit has been given you to guide you through life, to connect with you and to love on you. The Holy Spirit is the third person of the Godhead, and he is with you 24/7 throughout your life.

Prayer: Dear Heavenly Father, I thank and praise you for your constant presence with me through the Holy Spirit. You promise to never leave me and I trust you for your promise. Thank you that you are truth. Amen.

Journal

____
____
____
____
____

Day 83

For this reason, ever since I heard about your faith in the Lord Jesus and your love for all God's people, I have not stopped giving thanks for you, remembering you in my prayers. I keep asking that the God of our Lord Jesus Christ, the glorious Father, may give you the Spirit of wisdom and revelation so that you may know him better. Ephesians 1:15,16

This sounds strange from one who had spent a few years in Ephesus. He may be referring to a greatly enlarged church there, many of whom Paul did not know, or, if the book of Ephesians was intended as a circular letter. Whatever Paul's intention, we know Paul loves them and prays for them.

Check who is on your prayer list.

Prayer: Dear Heavenly Father, I pray for (*name the persons, and their issues or praises, who are on your prayer list*). Amen.

Journal

____

____

____

____

____

Day 84

I pray that the eyes of your heart may be enlightened in order that you may know the hope to which he has called you, the riches of his glorious inheritance in his holy people, and his incomparably great power for us who believe. Ephesians 1:17-19a

The eyes of the heart usually refers to the mind. He is praying for wisdom, revelation, and enlightenment for them, (and us).

My goodness, we certainly need those precious gifts to live in this age, don't we? Open your heart to all the Lord has for you and bow before him in joy and gratitude.

Prayer: Dear Heavenly Father, fill me with wisdom, revelation and enlightenment in my life as I live and serve those you have placed around me. Amen.

Journal

____

____

____

____

____

Day 85

That power is the same as the mighty strength, which he exerted when he raised Christ from the dead and seated him at his right hand in the heavenly realms, far above all rule and authority, power and dominion and every name that is invoked, not only in the present age but also in the one to come. Ephesians 1:19b-21

God is all powerful in the physical and supernatural worlds, we can see it in the resurrection of Christ Jesus, in his creation - which he spoke into being, his knowledge and in his plans. This same God is the one who has touched our life with unconditional love expressed through Christ Jesus.

Prayer: Dear Heavenly Father, I worship you today with a grateful heart. I love you with all my heart and soul, and I seek to serve you with all my being. Keep my mind on you so that I may see you, hear you and obey you. Amen.

Journal

____

____

____

____

____

Day 86

And God placed all things under his feet and appointed him to be head over everything for the church, which is his body, the fullness of him who fills everything in every way. Ephesians 1:22,23

'Under his feet' refers to the superiority of Christ Jesus and the destiny of the human race. He is the ultimate, powerful being who was, is and is to come - past, present and future. If we don't acknowledge him in this life, he will be known and acknowledged in the next life - however, to acknowledged only in the next life, means it is too late for salvation.

Today pray for loved ones and acquaintances who do not know Jesus as their personal Savior.

Prayer: Dear Heavenly Father, I pray for (*name the loved ones and acquaintances who do not know Jesus*) and ask you to open up their heart to you. Give me opportunities to tell them about you and how you have changed my life. Amen.

Journal

____

____

____

____

Day 87

As for you, you were dWead in your transgressions and sins, in which you used to live when you followed the ways of the world and of the ruler of the kingdom of the air, the spirit who is now at work in those who are disobedient. Ephesians 2:1,2

Paul describes the human life before meeting Jesus and becoming transformed. He describes us as having been 'dead' in our sins. This is a spiritual death. Jesus awakens us into spiritual life; through the price of sin he paid for us on the cross.

Prayer: Dear Heavenly Father, I raise my hands toward heaven and praise you for your redemption of my sin, and the adoption into your family. I love you back. Amen.

Journal

____

____

____

____

____

Day 88

All of us also lived among them at one time, gratifying the cravings of our flesh and following its desires and thoughts. Like the rest, we were by nature deserving of wrath. Ephesians 2:3

Also see Romans 1:18, 2:23, 9:23-29. Without Jesus and his sacrifice, we, the human race was doomed. Enter God's unconditional love and grace. Jesus entered this world to redeem us to himself, so we can live a life of freedom from sin's bondage for God's glory.

Prayer: Dear Heavenly Father, I praise you for freeing me from the chains of (*state the bondages*) which pulled me down low. I choose to live a life in total freedom and obedience to you, my Savior. Amen.

Journal

____

____

____

____

____

Day 89

But because of his great love for us, God, who is rich in mercy, made us alive with Christ even when we were dead in transgressions - it is by grace you have been saved. Ephesians 2:4,5

Have you considered this - even when we did not know Christ, he knew us, and he knew what was and is best for us? God's grace is enormous and forgiving. Grace is an unmerited gift. He overlooked our abhorrent sinful condition and loved on us, (he still does!), unconditionally and saved us through the power of the blood of Jesus Christ.

Oh, how we love him.

Prayer: Dear Heavenly Father, Oh how you loves me, you gave your life, what more could you give? Oh how I love you. Amen

Journal

____

____

____

____

____

Day 90

And God raised us up with Christ and seated us with him in the heavenly realms in Christ Jesus, in order that in the coming ages he might show the incomparable riches of his grace, expressed in his kindness to us in Christ Jesus. Ephesians 2:6,7

With Jesus living in our hearts, through salvation, we now follow a different path of life, one with a heart of obedience to our Lord. Pleasing Jesus is our joy and delight.

How is your heart today? Is Jesus your joy and delight? Can he shine his light through you? Honestly, Journal your responses to these questions.

Prayer: Dear Heavenly Father, I take your hand and walk with you. I walk in times and places of green pastures, and I also walk in the times and places of the shadow of death. Both, with my hand safely in yours. Thank you for always being with me. Amen.

Journal

____

____

____

____

____

Day 91

For it is by grace you have been saved, through faith - and this is not from yourselves, it is the gift of God - not by works, so that no one can boast. Ephesians 2:8,9

We have been made alive in the Spirit through an abundant gift of grace. It is a free, unmerited gift, fully given to us. We did not earn it, pay for it or obtain it any other way. It is given us through the power of the blood of Christ Jesus. Our heart is deeply thankful and full of sincere love toward the giver.

Prayer: Dear Heavenly Father, My heart is deeply thankful and full of sincere love towards you, the giver of salvation, to me an undeserving sinner. I love you. Amen.

Journal

Day 92

For we are God's handiwork, created in Christ Jesus to do good works, which God prepared in advance for us to do. Ephesians 2:10

Handiwork or workmanship, which means 'work of art'. God sees you as prized, spectacular, work or art, worth redeeming. He planned you, made you, redeemed you, is watching over you and has prepared a plan for your life. You matter to God; he made you with and for a purpose. This is a powerful verse.

Today, meditate on the truth of the words in this verse, and respond to God. Journal your thoughts.

Memorize Ephesians 2:10 and assimilate the meaning into your life.

Journal

____

____

____

____

____

Day 93

Therefore, remember that formerly you who are Gentiles by birth and called 'uncircumcised' by those who call themselves 'the circumcision' (which is done in the body by human hands) - remember that at that time you were separate from Christ, excluded from citizenship in Israel and foreigners to the covenants of the promise, without hope and without God in the world. But now, in Christ Jesus you who once were far away have been bought near by the blood of Christ. Ephesians 2:11-13

Wow, how impactful are these words to us! We were far from Christ, now we can hold his hand and sit on his lap - through the redemptive work of Christ Jesus. Praise his name.

Prayer: Dear Heavenly Father, what can I say, but Hallelujah. You have taken me from being a sinful person, to become a person 'saved by grace'. Your love did that for me and I am eternally grateful. Thank you so much. Amen.

Journal

____

____

____

____

____

Day 94

For he himself is our peace, who has made the two groups one and has destroyed the barrier, the dividing wall of hostility, by setting aside in his flesh the law with it's commandments and regulations. Ephesians 2:14,15a

Jesus broke down the division or barrier in a couple of ways - the barrier keeping humans from a righteous God, and the barrier between regenerated Jews and Gentiles. The broken barrier renders Jews and Gentiles united in faith. Interesting.

Prayer: Dear Heavenly Father, you are a God of miracles. You perform them all the time, we see many in your Holy Word, and we see them today. Keep my heart open to you that I may always see you with the eyes of my heart. Amen.

Journal

____

____

____

____

____

Day 95

His purpose was to create in himself one new humanity out of the two, thus making peace, and in one body to reconcile both of them to God through the cross, by which he put to death their hostility. He came and preached peace to you who were far away and peace to those who were near. For through him we both have access to the Father by one Spirit. Ephesians 2:15b-18

The phrase 'one new man' probably refers to the unity of believers, or the church. 'Their hostility' refers to the spirit which opposes the truth of unity in Christ. Christ put to death their hostility, and they became believers. He includes us in this concept since most of us are Gentiles. The mystery is that God created unity with Jews and Gentiles, which in itself is a miracle. Praise his name.

Prayer: Dear Heavenly Father, thank you for unity of Jews and Gentiles through the blood and resurrection of Jesus Christ, that we can be one in you. Thank you for your miracle power. Amen.

Journal

____

____

____

____

____

Day 96

Consequently, you are no longer foreigners and strangers, but fellow citizens with God's people and also members of his household, built on the foundation of the apostles and prophets with Christ Jesus himself as the chief cornerstone. Ephesians 2:19,20

The mention of the apostles and prophets indicate the solidity of the structure of God's salvation plan and ensuing unity of the church. The 'cornerstone' is the integral foundation of an ancient building which had been tested. Paul states that Jesus is the cornerstone of the Christian faith, on which our belief system is built.

Praise Jesus, he sees and knows you and calls you by name.

Prayer: Dear Heavenly Father, I am humbled that you see me and that you know my name. When I get to heaven you will look in my eyes and say my name. Wow. You, the cornerstone, the God of the universe, the King of Kings and the Lord of Lords, knows my name and are intricately interested in my live. I humbly thank you. Amen.

Journal

____

____

____

____

____

Day 97

In him the whole building is joined together and rises to become a Holy temple in the Lord. And in him you too are being build together to become a dwelling in which God lives by his Spirit. Ephesians 2:21,22

Have you noticed there is no past tense in these scriptures? God's building in our lives does not stop, it is ongoing as we live our lives in this world. We, his people are being built together as a place for the Holy Spirit to live, in us individually and corporately as a body, his church. He works his transforming power continually in our lives to make us to be more like Jesus - in our individual lives and in our corporate lives as part of his body - the church.

Prayer: Dear Heavenly Father, thank you for continually working on me and getting me there - please don't give us. Help me to be strong and courageous to let you in to do your work in me, as you rid me of the 'stuff' that are filthy rags in your site. Amen.

Journal

____

____

____

____

____

Day 98

For this reason I, Paul, the prisoner of Christ Jesus for the sake of you Gentiles - surely you have heard about the administration of God's grace that was given to me for you, that is, the mystery made known to me by revelation, as I have already written briefly. Ephesians 3:1-3

Paul takes a little hiatus here, to recap and allude to his visitation with Jesus on the road to Damascus and his time in Arabia where the Lord instructed him, and, as a prisoner for his efforts to preach Jesus. The message of the 'mystery' is often thought as being the unity of Jews and Gentiles, because of their united faith in Christ Jesus. This in itself is a miracle.

Prayer: Dear Heavenly Father, Is there any person you need to make peace with? Help me to hear your voice and lead me to situations where I can make amends with them.

Journal

____

____

____

____

____

Day 99

In reading this, then you will be able to understand my insight into the mystery of Christ, which was not made known to people in other generations as it has now been revealed by the Spirit of God's holy apostles and prophets. Ephesians 3:4,5

Paul is stating he is not the only one to receive the revelations, as the apostles and prophets had also been enlightened. This is the beauty of the Christian faith. We can find Jesus, the Messiah, described throughout the Old Testament, beginning in Genesis 3:18, and we see him revealed in the flesh in the New Testament. Now, in these verses his power of unity is revealed.

Prayer: Dear Heavenly Father, I love that you are Alpha and Omega, the beginning and end. I have hope and security knowing that nothing occurs without your eyes on it. Thank you for your superior and foreknowledge. I rest in you. Amen.

Journal

____

____

____

____

____

Day 100

This mystery is that through the gospel the Gentiles are heirs together with Israel, members together of one body and sharers together in the promise in Jesus Christ. Ephesians 3:6

Do you notice the word 'together' is used three times in this verse. Paul is making a point: unity is togetherness. Regenerated Gentiles become Spiritual Israel, giving them 'heir' status. We are heirs of God's promises and future. How amazing is He? Taking broken vessels, making them new and fit for the service of the King of Heaven.

Prayer: Dear Heavenly Father, you are an awesome God, you reign in heaven above with wisdom power and love. In you I rest, trust and hope. Amen.

Journal

____

____

____

____

____

Day 101

I became a servant of this gospel by the gift of God's grace given to me through the working of his power. Although I am less than the least of all the Lord's people, this grace was given to me: to preach to the Gentiles, the boundless riches of Christ... Ephesians 3:7,8a

Paul expresses his modesty as he describes God's grace toward him. The same grace was given to him by God's power - as God gives to us his grace through his power, also. God's grace is abundant and flowing. It gives us the zeal to reach others for the Lord.

Prayer: Dear Heavenly Father, thank you for your grace in my life. Let it flow through me to others. Amen.

Journal

____

____

____

____

Day 102

...and to make plain to everyone the administration of this mystery, which for ages past was kept hidden in God, who created all things. His intent was that now, through the church, the manifold wisdom of God should be made known to the rulers and authorities in the heavenly realms, according to his eternal purpose that he accomplished in Jesus Christ our Lord. Ephesians 3:8b-11

God performed a miracle by reconciling Jews and Gentiles through the his body, the church. Manifold means variegated or multifaceted. The miracle of reconciliation is observed on earth as well as in the heavens, with Jesus being the head of the church. Our miracle performing God is past, present and future. He still performs miracles today.

Prayer: Dear Heavenly Father, Thank you for the miracle you have performed in my life and in the lives of others with whom I am acquainted. (*Name those miracles*). Amen.

Journal

____

____

____

____

Day 103

In him and through faith in him we may approach God with freedom and confidence. I ask you, therefore, not to be discouraged by my sufferings for you, which are your glory. Ephesians 3:12,13

Jesus' sacrificial blood made the way for redeemed humans to have access to God. He became the mediator between God and man - 1 Timothy 2:15. Because we have asked Jesus to forgive our sins and have opened ourselves to his Lordship, he covers our sins with his blood. God no longer sees us as sinners but redeemed. Therefore, we have access to God through Christ Jesus, by his grace.

Prayer: Dear Heavenly Father, I am amazed and thankful for your perfect plan of salvation of the human race. Amen.

Journal

____
____
____
____

Day 104

For this reason, I kneel before the Father, from whom every family in heaven and on earth derives its name. I pray that out of his glorious riches he may strengthen you with power and through his Spirit in your inner being, so that Christ may dwell in your hearts, through faith. Ephesians 3:14-17a

Our Lord has opened his arms to us and adopted us into his family. He wants us to dwell with him in complete comfort and peace. Christ dwelling in our hearts indicates a total surrender of us to him: our attitudes, motives, thoughts and relationships. He sees who we are, what we do, say and think. Oh my!!

Prayer: Dear Heavenly Father, I praise you for your closeness to me. Thank you that you are an encouragement to me and that you lovingly guide me. Amen.

Journal

____

____

____

____

____

Day 105

And I pray that you, being rooted and established in the love, may have power, together with all the Lord's holy people, to grasp how wide and long and high and deep is the love of Christ, and to know this love that surpass knowledge - that you may be filled to the measure of all the fullness of God. Ephesians 3:17b-19

Love that surpasses knowledge is love that is given to us beyond what we can think or dream. It is so great we don't fully understand it, but it has been given to us to know. Our amazing, eternal, creative God reaches to you in his love. Accept Him into your day, your mind, your activities. Let him love on you.

Prayer: Dear Heavenly Father, I accept your vast and lavish love you pour over me. I invite you into my being, in all I so and say. I surrender it all to you. Amen.

Journal

____

____

____

____

____

Day 106

Now to him who is able to do immeasurably more than all we ask or imagine, according to his power that is at work within us, to him be glory in the church and in Christ Jesus throughout all generations, for ever and ever, Amen. Ephesians 3:20,21

This salvation is powerful, describing our Lord's unfailing, powerful attributes. His power is present with us today, in our lives, and in the lives of others. The unity of believers is seen in the body of Christ, the Church. His power should be seen in the Church today.

Watch the movie - "Jesus Revolution'

Prayer: Dear Heavenly Father, today I pray for the church, particularly for those who believe half truths or popular thinking, or who are not willing to take a deeper step toward you. Send us a revival. Amen.

Journal

____

____

____

____

____

Day 107

As a prisoner for the Lord, then, I urge you to live a life worthy of the calling you have received. Be completely humble and gentle, be patient, bearing with one another in love. Make every effort to keep the unity of the Spirit through the bond of peace. Ephesians 4:1-3

Paul is urging us to maintain the unity of the Spirit through the bond of peace. How do we do that? In God's strength and power, forgive each other, be caring and hospitable, care for the poor and needy, minister to each other, cry with each other, rejoice together.

Prayer: Dear Heavenly Father, thank you for those men and women (family, children) you have surrounded me with. You love each of them, help me to love them with your love. Help me to care for them, help me to see their needs and joys, so I may cry with them and rejoice with them. Amen.

Journal

____

____

____

____

____

Day 108

There is one body and one Spirit - just as you were called to one hope when you were called; one Lord, one faith, one baptism; one God and Father of all, who is over all and through all and in all. Ephesians 4:4-6

It is believed that baptism at Paul's time was a public affair, therefore it was a statement to others of the person's choice to follow Jesus. Today, it is often performed in a baptismal at Church, but some churches select to perform baptism at the beach, in a river or lake. Paul emphasizes, one Lord, one faith, one baptism - lest we become tempted to follow other thoughts or even include them into the Christian faith.

Prayer: Dear Heavenly Father, thank you for the unity we can have in you. We are one in the Spirit we are one in you Lord. Keep us hearing your voice together. Amen.

Journal

____

____

____

____

____

Day 109

But to each one of us grace has been given as Christ apportioned it.
Ephesians 4:7

Have you noticed how often our readings have included grace? Grace, being an unmerited gift which has been given to us as a freely. Because of grace, received through God's tender love towards us, we are adopted children in God's family through the work of the cross. Per Oxford Dictionary, 'Grace in Christian belief is the free and unmerited favor of God, as manifested in the salvation of sinners and bestowal of blessings.'

Prayer: Dear Heavenly Father, you are a God of blessings which you pour out on me, and your people. So many blessings, how can I count them all? I'll start with these (*speak your blessings with a grateful heart to your Lord and Savior*). Amen.

Journal

Day 110

This is why it says: when he ascended on high, he took many captives and gave gifts to his people.' (What does 'he ascended' mean except that he has also descended to the lower, earthly regions? He who descended is the very one who ascended higher than all the heavens in order to fill the whole universe.) Ephesians 4:8-10

Paul takes the opportunity to remind us of Psalm 68:18, where it describes Christ descending to earth and ascending to the heaven to fill the universe. It gives us the picture of an almighty God who can do anything. He is in full control of the universe. This means, in day-to-day terms, global warming, space exploration, intergalactic communication, etc, are in **HIS** control.

Prayer: Dear Heavenly Father, you are so big, so mighty, so powerful, there is nothing you cannot. The mountains are yours; the valleys are yours; the whole world is in your control. Hallelujah and amen.

Journal

Day 111

So Christ himself gave the apostles, the prophets, the evangelists, the pastors and teachers, to equip his people for the works of service, so that the body of Christ may be built up until we all reach unity in the faith and in the knowledge of the Son of God and become mature, attaining to the whole measure of the fullness of Christ. Ephesians 4:11-13

Romans 12:6-8 has a further listing of gifts from the Lord - serving, encouraging, contributing to others, leadership, mercy. Our Lord gives us gifts in order to share with others and create unity. The gifts are to 'prepare God's people for the works of service', and in some translations, the word 'equip' is used instead of 'prepare'.

Prayer: Dear Heavenly Father, I want to use the gifts you have bestowed on me to the fullest measure. Direct me to opportunities where you can use me, keep me in your will with a clean heart and pure attitude. Amen.

Journal

____

____

____

____

____

Day 112

Then we will no longer be infants tossed back and forth by the waves and blown here and there by every wind of teaching, and by the cunning and craftiness of people in their deceitful scheming. Ephesians 4:14

Gifts have been given to us to share with each other so we will be informed and strong in our faith as we spread the gospel to others and perform our work for the Lord. This, in turn, creates a unified, strong body of believers.

Do you identify Gifts of the Spirit in your life? If so, how do you use it/them? If not, ask the Lord to hone gifts in your life. Journal your discoveries and prayers.

Prayer: Dear Heavenly Father, Thank you for the gifts of (*name your gifts*) you have placed into my life. Help me to use them at your bidding with you. Keep me in your will. Amen.

Journal

____

____

____

____

____

Day 113

Instead, speaking the truth in love, we will grow to become in every respect the mature body of him who is the head, that is Christ. From him, the whole body, joined and held together by every supporting ligament, grows and builds itself in love, as each part does its work. Ephesians 4:15,16

Speaking the truth is sometimes difficult and/or painful. Adding love into the mix helps to make it a little easier to say or receive. The idea of a body with Christ as the head, and Christians as the working parts of the body through ministry gifts and fruit of the spirit, is a familiar imagery. The continuing functioning and acting of the body together leads to maturity.

Prayer: Dear Heavenly Father, You are amazing in your foresight, planning and purpose. Thank you for your body, the church. Thank you for ministry gifts and fruits of the Spirit. Thank you that you teach and lead us to people and situations where you want us to use our gifts. Help me to keep my ears open to your gentle leading. Amen.

Journal

____
____
____
____
____

Day 114

So, I tell you this, and insist on it in the Lord, that you must no longer live as the Gentiles do, in the futility of their thinking. They are darkened in their understanding and separated from the life of God, because of the ignorance that is in them due to the hardening of their hearts. Ephesians 4:17,18

The phrase, 'hardening of their hearts' punctuates the scriptural meaning of an unbeliever. It means an unresponsiveness towards God - probably deliberate. Though scripture does inform us that God hardens men's hearts, for example, Pharaoh, Exodus 9:12, most people's hearts are hardened through unbelief.

Prayer: Dear Heavenly Father, I pray for (*an unbelieving family member or others*), and ask that you will soften their hearts, so they can hear your voice and open themselves to the truth of the Gospel. Thank you. Amen.

Journal

____

____

____

____

____

Day 115

Having lost all sensitivity, they have given themselves over to sensuality so as to indulge in every kind of impurity, and they are full of greed. Ephesians 4:19

The hardening of the heart has consequences. This verse tells us that once sensitivity or absolutes are lost, people lust for more of the sensuous behaviors. We know that often the consequences are disease, broken families, crime, murder, depression, sadness, and so on - a path leading to unhappiness and hopelessness.

Prayer: Dear Heavenly Father, today, again I pray for our sad and confused world, and the folk in my life (*name them*) who are not in your family. I ask that you will soften their hearts so that they can hear about your love for them. Amen.

Journal

____

____

____

____

____

Day 116

That, however, is not the way of life you learned, when you heard about Christ and were taught in him in accordance with the truth that is in Jesus. You were taught, with regard to your former way of life, to put off your old self, which is being corrupted by its deceitful desires, to be made new in the attitude of your minds; and put on the new self, created to be like God in true righteousness and holiness. Ephesians 4:20-24

This is what we do in the sustaining power of the Holy Spirit - put off the old self and put on the new self. The act of 'putting off' is purposeful, like undressing from your night clothes, to get ready for the day; and 'putting on' also is purposeful, as if getting dressed for the day. This 'new self' is a new way of life, a life of truth, righteousness and holiness.

Prayer: Dear Heavenly Father, I purposely put off my old self, thank you for forgiving me of my old ways. I purposely put on my new self and am eager to learn your ways - ways of righteousness, truth and love. Amen.

Journal

____

____

____

____

____

Day 117

Therefore, each of you must put off falsehood and speak truthfully to your neighbor, for we are all members of one body. In your anger do not sin. Do not let the sun go down while you are still angry, and do not give the devil a foothold. Ephesians 4:25-27

Not all anger is sin, it is an emotion which needs to be submitted to the Lord. Paul's advice is worthy of heeding – 'do not let the sun go down while you are still angry.' The opposite of anger is forgiveness. Both anger and forgiveness are a choice.

Oh, that we develop the habit of choosing forgiveness - what a happier place the world would be! Less stress related illnesses, less violence, less murders.

Prayer: Dear Heavenly Father, I ask for strength to manage my emotions. I choose forgiveness over anger and hate - give me the courage and strength to forgive others as you forgave men. Amen.

Journal

____

____

____

____

____

Day 118

Anyone who has been stealing must steal no longer, but must work, doing something useful with their own hands, that they may have something to share with those in need. Ephesians 4:28

Most of us could say 'I don't steal, therefore this scripture doesn't refer to me'. But, did you take stationary from your work office? Did you eat food at the supermarket and not pay for it? Do you conveniently not tell the cashier they missed totaling up something in your basket? Did you take a bite of someone else's food?

Ask the Lord to reveal unsavory habits to you, confess and ask for forgiveness and healing. Use your new found freedom to help provide for others. Journal your prayer and outcome.

Prayer: Dear Heavenly Father, sometimes I am blind to my sinful nature, even though I am saved by grace. Enlighten me our of my denial and help me see where I need correction in my ways. Thank you. Amen.

Journal

____
____
____
____
____

Day 119

Do not let any unwholesome talk come out of your mouth, but only what is helpful for building others up according to their needs, that it may benefit those who listen. Ephesians 4:29

We are encouraged to exchange our speech from that which has a negative power, to that which is encouraging and wholesome. We can be assertive and loving in our words by beginning our sentences with 'I feel' or 'I sense' or 'I (naming whatever you need to put here)' and adding the qualifier to follow. For example, 'I feel delighted when you read stories to the kids, so I can get dinner on the table.' Use the 'I feel' or 'I sense' introduction to your sentence instead of starting a sentence with a challenging 'you' or 'why' which creates offense instantly. For example, 'You always leave your laundry on the floor.' That doesn't make anyone feel good.

Let your words be as 'apples of gold in settings of silver', Proverbs 25:11.

Prayer: Dear Heavenly Father, Help me to choose my words wisely when I communicate to others. I desire to love rather than create offense. Amen.

Journal

____

____

____

____

____

Day 120

And do not grieve the Holy Spirit, with whom you are sealed for the day of Redemption. Get rid of all bitterness, rage and anger, brawling and slander, along with every form of malice. Be kind and compassionate to one another, forgiving each other, just as in Christ God forgave you. Ephesians 4:30

These verses are another set to pray 'Search me O God and know my heart', Psalm 139:23. Open yourself to our Lord, and let him speak to you today. Follow his guidance.

Journal your prayer and the outcome.

Prayer: Dear Heavenly Father, Search me O God and know my heart today, test me and know my anxious thoughts. See if there is any offensive way in me, and lead me in the way everlasting. Amen.

Journal

____

____

____

____

____

Day 121

Follow God's example, therefore, as dearly loved children and walk in the way of love, just as Christ loved us and gave himself up for us as a fragrant offering and sacrifice to God. Ephesians 5:1,2

One way of imitating God is to have a forgiving spirit. The Lord's prayer states 'forgive us our debts as we also have forgiven our debtors', Matthew 6:12. Christianity is based on forgiveness. Forgiveness is a choice. How are you managing forgiving others and forgiving yourself? The 'fragrant offering' eludes to the Old Testament sacrificial system. However, Jesus was sacrificed on our behalf, once and for all - he is the 'fragrant offering'.

Prayer: Dear Heavenly Father, thank you for your forgiveness of my sins, and for cleansing me from all unrighteousness. Check my heart to see if there is any unforgiveness in me. Help me to forgive in the same manner you forgave me. Amen

Journal

____

____

____

____

____

Day 122

But among you there must not be even a hint of sexual immorality, or any kind of impurity, or of greed, because these are improper for God's holy people. Nor should there be any obscenity, foolish talk or coarse joking, which are out of place, but rather thanksgiving. Ephesians 5:3,4

Paul is calling out a depraved mind and asking us to check ourselves in our behavior and speech. He suggests being thankful instead of engaging in unseemly behaviors. If you have difficulty with this concept, ask the Lord for strength to disengage from those unseemly behaviors, and put upbuilding thoughts in your mind and speech, giving praise to our God.

Prayer: Dear Heavenly Father, Search my heart today. Show me the behaviors I exhibit which do not please you. Put a spirit of thankfulness in my heart, that I my shine your love to others throughout my day. Amen.

Journal

____

____

____

____

____

Day 123

For of this you can be sure: No immoral, impure or greedy person - such a person is an idolater - has any inheritance in the Kingdom of Christ and of God. Let no one deceive you with empty words, for because of such things God's wrath comes on those who are disobedient. Therefore, do no be partners with them. Ephesians 5:5-7

Even though we live in the world alongside unbelievers, our Lord does not want Christians to participate in their lifestyle. Their lifestyle replaces God with idols - maybe not images, but idols of money, sex, fashion, fame, food, drugs, alcohol and so on.

Prayer: Dear Heavenly Father, Keep my eyes on you and my ears hearing your voice and not the voice that would pull me away from you. Draw me to love the things that you love and lead me to serve you with all my heart.

Journal

____

____

____

____

____

Day 124

For you were once darkness, but now you are light in the Lord. Live as children of light, (for the fruit of the light consists of all goodness, righteousness and truth) and find out what pleases the Lord. Ephesians 5:8-10

During times of 'Light' or daylight, the world is productive - consider how nature grows in the sunlight, Vitamin D is obtained from the sun, humans are productive mostly during the day, etc. Our Lord wants us to live a productive life in the Light emanated from knowing and loving Christ Jesus. We are, in turn, to be a light set on a hill, a beacon of hope to a lost, sad world.

How does Jesus shine through you?

Prayer: Dear Heavenly Father, May I be that light on a hill, and the salt of the earth in all the encounters I have with others in my world. This little light of mine, I want to let it shine. Don't let satan blow it out, I want to let it shine. Hold it under a bushel, no! I want to let it shine - for others to see you shining out through me. Amen.

Journal

____

____

____

____

____

Day 125

Have nothing to do with the fruitless deeds of darkness but rather expose them. It is shameful even to mention what the disobedient do in secret. Ephesians 5:11,12

Our Lord wants us to live pure lives - morally, financially, spiritually. He has given us power to withstand the onslaughts of the enemy, through faith and trust in him, by the Holy Spirit, and through our conscience. In Ephesians 6, we will see the full spiritual armor in use.

Pray for the Lord to guard and protect you during times of temptation, to give you resolve.

Prayer: Dear Heavenly Father, thank you that there is no temptation given to me, that is not common to man. But you are faithful, and with that temptation you provide me a way of escape so that I may endure it. Thank you for the provision you give me to stand in faith. (1 Corinthians 10:13) Amen.

Journal

____
____
____
____
____

Day 126

But everything exposed by the light becomes visible - and everything that is illuminated becomes a light. This is why it is said: 'Wake up, sleeper, rise from the dead, and Christ will shine on you'. Ephesians 5:13,14

Paul uses the imagery of light exposing what is unseen. Christ is the Light of the World. He illuminates the darkness in our lives, so we can become aware of areas which need to be surrendered. Christians are meant to be the 'light of the world', Matthew 5:14,16, we are to be shining our light for Christ and expose darkness, or dark deeds.

How are you doing in this? Is your light shining in your family, at school, at work, in your day to day activities? Journal what you observe and place your observations before the altar.

Prayer: Dear Heavenly Father, I ask for you to shine in me and through me. May I be that light on a hill for others to see you because of the transformation you are working in me and your powerful healing of my soul. Amen.

Journal

____

____

____

____

____

Day 127

Be very careful, then, how you live - not as unwise but as wise, making the most of every opportunity, because the days are evil. Therefore, do not be foolish, but understand what the Lord's will is. Ephesians 5:15-17

Paul is reminding us to keep in step with the Holy Spirit and seize opportunities he sends our way to represent Jesus. They include: kind words and attitudes, doing good, helping others, speaking words of wisdom and peace - you add to the list.

Look for those God given opportunities in your day today and subsequent weeks. Journal what you are quickened to do or say and Journal the outcome.

Prayer: Dear Heavenly Father, thank you for your presence which is always with me. Thank you that you prompt me, guide me, suggest to me, and Kindly guide me toward the ways you want me to go, and to speak the words you want me to speak. I trust you. Amen.

Journal

____

____

____

____

____

Day 128

Do not get drunk on wine which leads to debauchery. Instead, be filled with the Spirit, speaking to one another with psalms, hymns and songs from the Spirit. Sing and make music in your heart to the Lord, always giving thanks to God the Father for everything, in the name of our Lord Jesus Christ. Ephesians 5:18-20

This is another comparison. Paul suggests - instead of getting drunk with wine, be filled with the Holy Spirit. Don't you enjoy his suggestion - sing to each other, giving thanks to God, making music in your heart.

Have you done this? Today, spend time in thankfulness and making music in your heart. Create a list of songs and thanks in case you run out or your mind draws a blank.

Today, spend time singing your favorite praise songs to the Lord, making music in your heart.

Journal

Day 129

Submit to one another out of reverence to Christ. Wives submit yourselves to your own husbands as you do to the Lord. For the husband is the head of the wife as Christ is the head of the church, his body, of which he is the Savior. Now as the church submits to Christ, so also wives should submit to their husbands in everything. Ephesians 5:21-24

In our day and age, there are so many different relationships: marriage, defacto marriage, single parenthood, singleness, abusive relationships - so how does one interpret the verse? Simple, if there is an absentee husband (physically or emotionally), Christ stands in his place. If there is a functioning husband, submission is qualified by 'as in the Lord'. We all are to submit to the Lord. Some commentaries suggest that the greek grammar indicates that this mutual submission is associated with the filling of the Spirit. Also see a description of the Wife of Noble Character in Proverbs 31:10-31.

Prayer: Dear Heavenly Father, keep my heart and mind open to submission to you, and my husband (*if you have one*), just as you have asked we do. Amen.

Journal

____

____

____

____

____

Day 130

Husbands, love your wives, just as Christ loved the church and gave himself up for her, to make her holy, cleansing her by the washing with water through the word, and to present her to himself, as a radiant church, without stain or wrinkle or any other blemish, but holy and blameless. Ephesians 5:25-27

Wives are compared to the church. Christ loves the church and is lovingly developing her to Spiritual maturity. Husbands are to love their wives as Christ loved the church.

Prayer: Dear Heavenly Father, I pray for my husband (*or pray for husbands you know if you are not married*), asking you to strengthen their love for you and love for their wives. Amen.

Journal

____

____

____

____

____

Day 131

In the same way husbands ought to love their wives as their own bodies. He who loves his wife loves himself. After all, no one ever hated his own body, but they feed and care for their body, just as Christ does the church - for we are members of his body. Ephesians 5:28-30

The Biblical premise of marriage is: two people becoming one unit, or part of each other. With the 'logical' thinking patterns of a man, and the 'global' thinking patterns of a woman, the unit is enhanced and complete. Bringing children into the world with this environment (that is if it is working as it should), should provide a safe haven to nurture them and develop them into strong men and women.

Prayer: Dear Heavenly Father, thank you for your concept and plan of marriage. I pray for marriages in this world that have broken down. Marriages without you, and marriages where there is abuse. I ask you apply your healing balm to (*speak of the unhealthy marriages you know about*) and draw the husband and wife to you for healing. Amen.

Journal

____
____
____
____
____

Day 132

For this reason, a man will leave his father and mother and be united to his wife, then the two will become one flesh. This is a profound mystery - but I am talking about Christ and the Church. However, each one of you, must love his wife as he loves himself, and the wife must respect her husband. Ephesians 5:31-33

The Bible portrays the church as being the 'bride of Christ'. Marriage is a sacred institution to God, as we can see by the parallels made here. Husbands are to love their wives as they love themselves, and the wives are to respect their husbands.

Prayer: Dear Heavenly Father, I pray for marriage, my own (*if you are married*), my parents, my friends and their parents, my relatives and my neighbors. May the two parties grow and mature in their love and their mutual respect they have for each other.

Journal

____

____

____

____

____

Day 133

Children, obey your parents in the Lord, for this is right. Honor your father and mother - which is the first commandment with a promise - so that it may go well with you and that you may enjoy a long life on earth. Ephesians 6:1-3

Our Lord's imagery of a family is specific here. We are part of his spiritual family, but we also have a natural, physical family with parents and probably siblings. God wants us to honor and obey our parents. The honor and respect is lifelong. We need each other no matter which stage of life we are in.

Dear Heavenly Father, I pray for my parents and my siblings (*name each of them*). May we care for each other always. Repair the difficult things that may or may not have arisen between us so we can all be of one mind. I pray for my family members who do not know you, that you will draw them by your love and mighty power. Amen.

Journal

____

____

____

____

Day 134

Fathers, do not exasperate your children; instead bring them up in the training and instruction of the Lord. Ephesians 6:4

Fathers must surrender any right they feel they have to act unreasonably toward their children. Even though parents created their children, they have the responsibility to care, future and guide them, but not 'own' them or treat them as commodities. Children are humans with dreams, needs, wants, but they are not 'things' to be mistreated or tossed away.

Prayer: Dear Heavenly Father, I pray for the missing, abused, trafficked and unloved children in this sad world or sin, vice and evil. Thank you for groups like *(name rescue groups)* which help to restore these children and rehabilitate them back into normal society. I pray for your intervention into the lives of these dear ones. Amen.

Journal

____

____

____

____

Day 135

Slaves, obey your earthly masters with respect and fear, and with sincerity of heart, just as you would obey Christ. Obey them not only to win their favor when their eye is on you, but as slaves of Christ, doing the will of God from your heart. Serve wholeheartedly, as if you were serving the Lord, not people, because you know that the Lord will reward each one for whatever good they do, whether they are slave or free. Ephesians 6:5-8

These verses also refer to our work or institutions, e.g., toward bosses or teachers, not just as to slaves. No matter our situation, choose to work to your best ability, as if you were working for Christ, which you are. Check your attitudes and motives.

Prayer: Dear Heavenly Father, Keep my attitudes to my work wholesome - work being a career, occupation or schoolwork. Help me in difficult situations where I am being misjudged or maligned, keep me true to you, I rest and trust in you to look after me. Amen.

Journal

____

____

____

____

____

Day 136

And masters, treat your slaves in the same way. Do not threaten them, since you know that he who is both their master and yours is in heaven, and there is no favoritism with him. Ephesians 6:9

It was tricky in those days with slaves and masters, because often, both were Christians. The book of Philemon is an example of this. However, in our days masters are like our bosses or instructors. We all, no matter what level of the hierarchy we are, are to treat each other with kindness, honor and respect.

Prayer: Dear Heavenly Father, Help me exhibit you in my life as I manage my day at school, or, work. Keep me in your will so I will be that shining light for you. Amen.

Journal

____

____

____

____

____

Day 137

Finally, be strong in the Lord and in his mighty power. Put on the full armor of God so that you can take your stand against the devil's schemes. Ephesians 6:10,11

Our attention is turned to the spiritual battle for our lives. First and foremost, we are reminded that God's power is invincible and is available to us to take, use and triumph. Following the reminder, Paul tells us to put on the spiritual armor. Even though the armor is described as what is available in about AD 60, in our day there are many similarities. This armor is to help us to stand against the devil's evil schemes and protect our life.

Prayer: Dear Heavenly Father, You are all powerful, all knowing, supreme, Alpha and Omega, King of Kings, Lord of Lord, Prince of Peace, the Creator of the World. I trust in you to keep me safe from the devil's evil schemes. Amen.

Journal

____

____

____

____

____

Day 138

For our struggle is not against flesh and blood, but against the rulers, against the authorities and against the powers of this dark world and against the spiritual forces of evil in the heavenly realms. Ephesians 6:10,11

This battle for us is a spiritual battle, which means our real enemy is the devil, not just those things he uses to make life uncomfortable and difficult. Spiritual warfare uses spiritual weapons. Spiritual weapons include: belief in Jesus Christ, christian faith, trust in the Lord, God's word, fasting, exorcisms, the mighty name of Jesus, and prayer.

Today, think about the battles you face, and together with Christ continue to use your spiritual weapons for deliverance.

Prayer: Dear Heavenly Father, I think of the battles I face. The battles of *(name them)*. With you at my side and the weapons of spiritual warfare you provide, together we will be successful. Thank you for all that you do for me. I love you. Amen.

Journal

____

____

____

____

____

Day 139

Therefore, put on the full armor of God, so that when the day of evil comes, you may be able to stand your ground, and after you have done everything, to stand. Ephesians 6:13

In context, the armor Paul is about to explain is Roman style. However, throughout history we see many styles of armor, but they each have protection for the head and chest and feet, plus their armament is complimented with weapons. This gives the wearer protection of their body from the onslaught of the enemy as well as weaponry with which to fight off the onslaught. Paul urges us to wear the spiritual armor for our protection from the evil schemes of the devil and the weapons of warfare to ward off the offense.

Prayer: Dear Heavenly Father, you think of everything for us. You have provided a way in which we can ward off the enemy, from every part of our being. In your name demons will have to flee. (Mark 1:21-23). Hallelujah! Amen.

Journal

____

____

____

____

____

Day 140

Stand firm then, with the belt of truth buckled around your waist, with the breastplate of righteousness in place and with your feet fitted with the readiness that comes from the gospel of peace. Ephesians 6:13

A belt holds together a piece of clothing, hence the belt of truth providing the foundation of the Christian belief. A breastplate protects the vital organs in the thoracic cavity, signifying the attitude of righteousness or right living. Footwear is important as it will either hinder or advance a person's motility. Protecting feet in the spiritual context, enables a person to continue with spreading the good news of peace - the Gospel.

Prayer: Dear Heavenly Father, I put on the belt of truth, the breastplate of righteousness, and shoes for the spreading of your perfect Gospel. Keep me strong in the battle agains the forces of evil which seek to destroy me. Thank you for your love and power in my life. Amen.

Journal

____

____

____

____

____

Day 141

In addition to all this, take up the shield of faith with which you can extinguish all the flaming arrows of the evil one. Ephesians 6:16

Faith is belief - such as you believe that a chair will hold you up when you sit on it. Faith in the Godhead is acting upon God's promises he has made to you. Such as his promised power in your life, his omniscience, ever presence, all knowing, all loving and caring, and very importantly, He knows you by name. Your belief in and acceptance of salvation through the blood of Jesus, and forgiveness of your sins make you a target for the arrows of the evil one.

Prayer: Dear Heavenly Father, I praise you for you have already defeated the devil on the cross and by your resurrection. I you I have that power to defeat the enemy, by your name and your precious blood shed for me. Wow, and thank you. Amen.

Journal

____

____

____

____

____

Day 142

Take the helmet of salvation and the sword of the spirit which is the word of God. Ephesians 6:17

A helmet protects the control center of the body - the brain. The sword of the spirit is God's holy word, which is described throughout the Bible - see Psalm 119:11, 105, Hebrews 4:12. May we live to cherish God's word, learn it and live by it. It is living, up to date and deals with all aspects of human life, you into a deeper relationship with the one whose word it is - God.

Prayer: Dear Heavenly Father, I love your word. Help me to read it, assimilate it into my life, memorize it and use it as a weapon against the evil one. Amen.

Journal

____

____

____

____

____

Day 143

And pray in the spirit on all occasions with all kinds of prayers and requests. With this in mind, be alert and always keep on praying for all the Lord's people. Ephesians 6:18

Paul is suggesting that we pray with the help of the spirit. Often, we do not know what to pray for or how to pray effectively, but the Spirit leads us, and lays items or thoughts on our heart. We are to pray all kinds of prayers on all occasions. It is like having a prayerful attitude. The types of prayer we might pray could be petition, thankfulness, intercessory, conversational, healing, heavenly language, the Lord's prayer, or others.

Prayer: Today pray the Lord's prayer found in Matthew 6:5-15.

Journal

____

____

____

____

____

Day 144

Pray also for me, that whenever I speak, words may be given me so that I will fearlessly make known the mystery of the gospel for which I am an ambassador in chains. Pray that I may declare it fearlessly as I should.
Ephesians 6:19,20

This is our prayer as well, that we fearlessly speak the gospel wherever we are and in whatever we do for him. May our Lord grant you the gracious words to proclaim the wonderful truth of the gospel of Jesus Christ wherever you are in your life.

Prayer: Dear Heavenly Father may the words of my mouth and the meditation of my heart be acceptable to you. May whatever comes out of my mouth be wholesome, kind, truthful and loving. Please help me guard my mind and my mouth with your power. Amen.

Journal

____

____

____

____

____

Day 145

Tychicus, the dear brother and faithful servant in the Lord, will tell you everything, so that you also may know how I am and what I am doing. I am sending him to you for this very purpose, so that you may know how we are, and that he may encourage you. Ephesians 6:21,22

Tychicus is In Paul's network of faithful friends. He's the messenger from Paul to his beloved Ephesian church, with information about the spread of the gospel in Rome where Paul is in prison, as well as the wellbeing of Paul.

Prayer: Dear Heavenly Father, I pray for the wellbeing of *(name your friends and family)*. I pray for their continued spiritual growth and outworking of your plan in their lives. Thank you. Amen.

Journal

____

____

____

____

____

Day 146

Peace to the brothers and sisters, and love with faith from God the Father and the Lord Jesus Christ. Grace to all who love our Lord Jesus Christ with an undying love. Ephesians 6:23,24

Would you like a salutation like this from your friends? It is very loving. Asking for peace, love, faith and grace. How do you cherish your friends, family and acquaintances? Do you love on them, pray for them, keep in touch with them?

Prayer: Dear Heavenly Father, I ask you to give me knowledge and understanding in my relationships so I will be a godly example to friends and family as I care for them and about them.

Journal

____

____

____

____

____

Day 147

Paul and Timothy, servants of Christ Jesus, to all God's holy people in Christ Jesus at Philippi, together with overseers and deacons. Grace and peace to you from God our Father and the Lord Jesus Christ. Philippians 1:1,2

There is no doubt who the letter was from and who the letter was to. Philippi was a Roman frontier city in Asia Minor, many residents being retired Roman military men. The letter was written while Paul was a Roman prisoner. He loves to commend his readers with words such as 'grace and peace'.

How do you greet your friends? What words do you say to them? Do they feel uplifted when they are with you?

Prayer: Dear Heavenly Father, may I always speak wholesome, truthful, kind words to my family and friends, and those who cross my path. Amen

Journal

____

____

____

____

____

Day 148

I thank God every time I remember you. In all my prayers for all of you, I always pray with joy because of your partnership in the Gospel from the first day until now... Philippians 1:3-5

Loving words to loving people who have been kind to Paul. His primary reason in writing this letter was to thank them for a 'gift' they sent him, but he also uses this occasion to address some issues as we will see as we read through the chapters.

Let us use Paul's example by thanking God for our friends. In your Journal, list your friends and write beside their name, how they bless you.

Prayer: Dear Heavenly Father, thank you for my friends and family. Thank you for the ways they bless me. May I be a blessing to them as well. Thank you. Amen.

Journal

____

____

____

____

____

Day 149

...being confident of this, that he who began a good work in you will carry it on to completion until the day of Christ Jesus. Philippians 1:6

Here is a verse to learn by heart, to quote to yourself and to others for times when encouragement is needed. The Lord's work in us is 'good', meaning positive, life changing, healthy, cleansing, and, he continues his work in us until we see him in glory - he doesn't stop. How is that for unconditional love?

Today, rest in his love for you, bask in his presence, let him have full range in your life - see the adventures he has for you.

Memorize this verse.

Journal

____

____

____

____

____

Day 150

It is right for me to feel this way about all of you, since I have you in my heart, and whether I am in chains or defending and confirming the gospel, all of you share in God's grace with me. God can testify how I long for all of you with the affection of

Christ Jesus. Philippians 1:7,8

Even though these retired Roman military personal and other Christians in Philippi knew of Paul's detention by Rome, they still loved on him and sent his friend to him with their financial gift. Paul expresses his love toward them in verse 8.

How do you express love to your fellow man - at home, school, work or play?

Prayer: Dear Heavenly Father, Help me to hear and see with ears and eyes of faith, so I can be cognizant of the needs of those around me. Show me ways I can love on them. Amen.

Journal

____

____

____

____

____

Day 151

And this is my prayer, that your love may abound more and more in knowledge and depth of insight, so that you may be able to discern what is best and may be pure and blameless for the day of Christ, filled with the fruit of righteousness that comes through Jesus Christ - to the glory and praise of God. Philippians 1:9-11

This is Paul's prayer of blessing to the church of Philippi. Paul is praying for their Christian growth and discernment, so they can live a Christ-like life through belief in Christ Jesus.

May you feel the power of his prayer in your life as well.

Prayer: Dear Heavenly Father, I take Paul's prayer to the Philippians into my life as well. Help me to abound in knowledge and discernment so I may grow to be pure and blameless in your sight. Thank you. Amen.

Journal

____

____

____

____

____

Day 152

Now I want you to know, brothers and sisters, that what has happened to me has actually served to advance the Gospel. As a result, it has become clear throughout the whole palace guard and to everyone else, that I am in chains for Christ. Philippians 1:12,13

Throughout the palace guard it was clear that Paul was not imprisoned for a crime, but because of his love, belief and servitude for Christ Jesus. It was the jealous Jewish leaders who stirred up trouble to get him imprisoned. However, as we will read, Paul used this time to promote the Gospel to fellow prisoners and guards. What an amazing man - he used the opportunity he was in to extend the Kingdom of God.

How does your life reflect Jesus, especially in difficult spots?

Prayer: Dear Heavenly Father, Show me opportunities to share you with those around me. Give me the words of wisdom and courage to step out for you and speak to people about you and to pray for them. Thank you. Amen.

Journal

____

____

____

____

____

Day 153

And because of my chains, most of the brothers and sisters have become confident in the Lord and dare all the more to proclaim the gospel without fear. Philippians 1:14

Paul's situation encouraged others to speak of Jesus fearlessly, and there was an expansion of the Kingdom of God. Interesting isn't it? So often God takes a situation which is going 'south' and plasters it with his power which turns it around. Even though Paul was not released immediately, other Christians carried on preaching, thus birthing their evangelistic ministry.

He has the power to turn things around for you as well.

Prayer: Dear Heavenly Father,

Journal

____

____

____

____

____

Day 154

It is true that some preach Christ out of envy and rivalry, but others out of goodwill. The latter do so in love, knowing that I am put here for the defense of the gospel. The former preach Christ out of selfish ambition, not sincerely, supposing they can stir up trouble for me while I am in chains.
Philippians 1:15-17

Paul is referring to people who were out to make trouble for him, noting that their preaching of the gospel was with the wrong attitude or a competitive spirit. However, it didn't matter to him, because the gospel was still being preached.

Have you been persecuted by others because of your belief in Christ? Journal your experience and praise God for the outcome.

Prayer: Dear Heavenly Father,

Journal

____
____
____
____
____

Day 155

But what does it matter? The important thing is that in every way, whether from false motives or true, Christ is preached. And because of this I rejoice. Yes, I will continue to rejoice... Philippians 1:18

The gospel is not subject to man's attitudes as its validity or truth is far beyond man. Paul rejoiced because the gospel was being preached to more people through those who were true and honest Christians, as well as those who felt competitive towards Paul. Praise God for Paul's attitude of joy in the midst of being in chains, against his will.

How does this verse relate to you? Journal your thoughts.

Prayer: Dear Heavenly Father, Thank you for your message of hope to a sad and hopeless world. Thank you for working on me to gain my attention and for penetrating my heart with your message of hope to me. May I be an ambassador of the gospel in my day to day life as I live for you. Amen.

Journal

Day 156

…for I know that through your prayers and God's provision of the Spirit of Jesus Christ, what happened to me will turn out for my deliverance. I eagerly expect and hope that I will in no way be ashamed, but will have sufficient courage so that now as always Christ will be exalted in my body, whether by life or by death. Philippians 1:19,20

Today we will think about applying the phrase 'exalted in my body'.

How do you exalt Christ in your body? How do you express praise to the Lord? How do you love on your neighbors? Do you like your body and your actions? Do you praise God in your habits? Ponder these concepts. Journal your responses and pray over them.

Prayer: Dear Heavenly Father, Keep me true to you Lord Jesus. Keep me true in the race of life that I must run. Give me power, every hours to be true. Amen.

Journal

____

____

____

____

____

Day 157

For to me, to live is Christ and to die is gain. If I am to go on living in the body, this will mean fruitful labor for me. Yet, what shall I choose? I do not know! Philippians 1:21,22

It is clear that in Paul's mind, his imprisonment could lead to death. Here he talks about his thoughts, stating he would carry on the 'fruitful labor' of evangelism if he did live. But, he would also love to be with his Lord.

Prayer: Dear Heavenly Father, I pray for my family, friends, fellow students/workmates, neighbors and those whom I meet as I live my life. Let my life shine for you as a light or beacon on a hill, drawing people to you. Amen.

Journal

____

____

____

____

____

Day 158

I am torn between the two: I desire to depart and be with Christ, which is better by far; but it is more necessary for you that I remain in the body. Convinced of this, I know that I will remain, and I will continue with all of you for your progress and joy in the faith, so that through my being with you again your boasting in Christ Jesus will abound on account of me. Philippians 1:23-26

As we read, Paul deliberated over where he wanted to be, preferably with Christ. He was ready to be with Jesus, whom he met on the way to Damascus. See Acts 9:1-17. His conclusion to his argument was that he chose to be with 'them' to help in their christian growth. He was released to be with Jesus at the culmination of his second imprisonment during the persecution under Nero.

Prayer: Dear Heavenly Father, we all long to be with you, as you have saved us and given us eternal life as a promise. May I be found working for you in righteousness, when that day comes. Amen.

Journal

____

____

____

____

____

Day 159

Whatever happens, conduct yourselves in a manner worthy of the Gospel of Christ. Then, whether I come and see you or only hear about you in my absence, I will know that you stand firm in the one Spirit, striving together as one for the faith of the gospel without being frightened in any way by those who oppose you. Philippians 1:27-28a

Unity of the 'brethren' or 'brotherhood' is an amazing and healthy occurrence. Paul is encouraging them, through this letter, to continue together in the faith of the Gospel.

How is unity working in your life? Journal areas where unity needs to be enriched, then pray and praise God for his answers.

Prayer: Dear Heavenly Father, thank you that we are one in the spirit and one in the you. Others will know we are christians by our love, our love for you and our love for each other. Amen.

Journal

____

____

____

____

____

Day 160

This is a sign to them that they will be destroyed, but that you will be saved - and that by God. For it has been granted you on behalf of Christ not only to believe in him, but also to suffer for him, since you are going through the same struggle you saw I had and now hear I still have. Philippians 1:28b-30

These Christians were aware of the opposition and sufferings when Paul and Silas were opposed and thrown into jail. See Acts 16:16-40. Also, Paul's letter to the church in Philippi was written while he was a Roman prisoner. Persecution refines our faith - we either crumble or press in deeper.

Have you, or are you experiencing persecution? Journal your situation and praise God for helping you grow through it.

Prayer: Dear Heavenly Father, You are my shield and my song. It is you I run to in times of trouble and you I hold on to when I pass through the valley of the shadow of death. It is with you I lie down in green pastures and am refreshed. Thank you for caring about me.

Journal

____

____

____

____

____

Day 161

Therefore, if you have any encouragement from being united with Christ, if any comfort from his love, if any common sharing in the Spirit, if any tenderness and compassion, then make my joy complete by being like-minded, having the same love, being one in spirit and of one mind. Philippians 2:1,2

Being in and with Christ is to be in intimate personal relationship with him. From this relationship flow all the particular benefits and fruits of Salvation, like encouragement, goodness, peace, joy.

Isn't he wonderful?

Prayer: Dear Heavenly Father, thank you for your all-encompassing love and care for me, today, tonight and always - eternally. Amen.

Journal

____

____

____

____

____

Day 162

Do nothing out of selfish ambition or vain conceit. Rather, in humility, value others above yourselves.... Philippians 2:3

Selfish ambition is listed amongst the acts of the sinful nature in Galatians 5:20. Christians are to live a life of service and Christian love, preferring God and others over self. Joy is a fruit of the Spirit, Galatians 5:22. Joy is also an acronym for

Jesus, Others, You.

During your day today, look for opportunities to prefer others more than yourself. At the end of the day, Journal your experiences and Praise God for them.

Prayer: Dear Heavenly Father, What a wonderful day which is set aside looking for ways which I can 'prefer' or 'love on' others around me. I am very excited about performing 'random acts of kindness' for those around me. Show me those who particularly need to be loved. Amen.

Journal

____

____

____

____

____

Day 163

...not looking at own interests but each of you to the interests of others.
Philippians 2:4

Again, Paul is urging Christians to prefer others over themselves, and not the other way around.

How does this look in your life? These acts of selflessness come in many forms - at work, home, school, recreation. Do some self-reflection and Journal opportunities to purposely prefer others. Go and do these, then Journal what you did and felt, and the responses of others.

Prayer: Dear Heavenly Father, Again I am going to undertake 'random acts of kindness' toward those around me. Please direct me to the hurting ones, or those with hard attitudes, so you can love them through me. Amen.

Journal

____
____
____
____
____

Day 164

In your relationships with one another, have the same mindset as Christ Jesus: Who, being in very nature of God, did not consider equality with God something to be used to his own advantage, rather, he made himself nothing, taking the very nature of a servant, being made in human likeness. Philippians 2:5-7

Jesus' humility took his attitude from being equal with God to that of a humble servant. Jesus set the example for us - to humble ourselves before him and others, to serve him and our fellow mankind. History shows Christian service in many Humanitarian missions and organizations began with humble Christian beginnings, and with the promise of glorifying God. For example, orphanages throughout the world, World Vision, Harvard, YMCA, Doctors without Borders - you can add to the list.

What does your humility look like? Journal your thoughts and prayers.

Prayer: Dear Heavenly Father, I always want to showcase you and not me. It's all about you and not me - I am the vehicle you use to spread your message. May there be more of you and less of me. Amen.

Journal

Day 165

And being found in appearance as a man, he humbled himself and became obedient to death - even death on a cross! Therefore, God exalted him to the highest place and gave him the name that is above every name.....
Philippians 2:8,9

Because Jesus is God, he could have used his power to crush his oppressors, but he didn't. Instead, he had you and I in mind, and he went ahead with the redemptive plan of death and paid the price for us so we could be free from sin. This is the plan of salvation. Because of his obedience to his Father, God, he is exalted in the heavens and on the earth.

Write your salvation experience in your Journal, and share it with someone today.

Prayer: Dear Heavenly Father, Thank you for saving me and taking me from those awful depths of sin. Thank you for restoring me, by your blood and resurrection, and freeing me to live a life which pleases you. Amen.

Journal

____

____

____

____

____

Day 166

....that at the name of Jesus every knee should bow, in heaven, and on earth and under the earth, and every tongue acknowledge that Jesus Christ is Lord to the glory of God the Father. Philippians 2:10,11

God's desire and design is that everyone is saved, by redemption through the sacrifice of Jesus Christ. In love and gratefulness we bow ourselves and worship him.

How do you incorporate the worship of Jesus Christ into your day-to-day life? Think about this and practice it today. Journal your experiences.

Prayer: Dear Heavenly Father, I love you and I lift my voice to worship you, I rejoice in you, my Lord, in what you have done for me. Let me be a sweet sound in your ear.

Journal

____

____

____

____

____

Day 167

Therefore, my dear friends, as you have always obeyed - not only in my presence, but now much more in my absence, continue to work out your salvation with fear and trembling, for it is God who works in you to will and to act in order to fulfill his good purpose. Philippians 2:12,13

Salvation is an ongoing experience, thus Paul encourages the saints to 'work our your salvation'. It is a gift which needs to be honed, grown and matured.

How do you see your salvation experience growing in your life? Have you had to lay some of your attitudes or habits on the altar before the Lord? Journal this experience and the outcomes.

Prayer: Dear Heavenly Father, I entrust my transformation toward righteousness, solely to you because I trust and honor you. I am so glad that you are continually working on and in me - keep me in tune with your still small voice whispering to me. Amen.

Journal

____

____

____

____

____

Day 168

Do everything without grumbling or arguing, so that you may become blameless and pure children of God, without fault in a warped and crooked generation. Then you will shine among them like stars in the sky as you hold firmly to the word of life. Philippians 2:14-16a

Some of the issues of 'working out our salvation' include not complaining, arguing, nor unbelief, but instead becoming blameless and faultless by doing God's will. Christians should shine for goodness in a dark world, see Matthew 5:14.

Prayer: Dear Heavenly Father, I pray to day for strength and power to manage my attitudes and my tongue, so I will shine for you. May my attitudes and speech be wholesome, kind, honest and gentle. Amen.

Journal

____

____

____

____

____

Day 169

And then I will be able to boast on the day of Christ that I did not run or labor in vain. But even if I am being poured out like a drink offering on the sacrifice and service coming from your faith, I am glad and rejoice with all of you. So you too should be glad and rejoice with me. Philippians 2:16b-18

Paul could be referring to his imprisonment and subsequent martyrdom by his comment 'being poured out'. It could also be a reference to the drink offering in the Old Testament offerings, see Exodus 29:38-41. Paul loved his fellow Christians and converts, and encourages them to keep the faith, despite oppositions. It is a current message for us today as well - reminding us to continue to shine for Jesus and bask in the continuing work of salvation.

Prayer: Dear Heavenly Father, I choose to run this race of life with you leading and guiding me, despite the fiery darts of the enemy. I choose to keep my focus on you. Amen.

Journal

____

____

____

____

Day 170

I hope in the Lord Jesus to send Timothy to you soon, that I also may be cheered when I receive news about you. I have no one else like him, who will show genuine concern for your welfare. For everyone looks out for his own interests, not those of Christ Jesus. Philippians 2:19-21

Timothy is like a son to Paul and he has Paul's trust. Thus Paul commends him highly to the church in Philippi.

Do you have people in your life like Timothy? Are you a Timothy to someone?

Prayer: Dear Heavenly Father, I ask for you to lead me so my life is sincere and purposeful for your Kingdom. Lead me to a Timothy, or may I be a Timothy to someone. Amen.

Journal

Day 171

But you know that Timothy has proved himself because as a son with his father he has served me in the work of the gospel. I hope therefore, to send him as soon as I see how things go with me. And I am confident in the Lord that I myself will come soon. Philippians 2:22-24

Paul continues to describe his trust in Timothy and builds his image for acceptance by the church in Philippi. Paul is eager to hear of and see the growth of his converts. Timothy is the trusted representative he plans to send, in order to encourage them on Paul's behalf.

Do you mentor fellow christians in the faith, or , are you mentored by a committed Christian? Who are your friends? Journal your responses.

Prayer: Dear Heavenly Father, May I be a mentor, walking with another person in their walk with you. May I have a mentor to walk beside me in my life with you? Amen

Journal

____

____

____

____

____

Day 172

But I think it is necessary to send back to you Epaphroditus, my brother, co-worker and fellow soldier, who is also your messenger whom you sent to take care of my needs. For he longs for all of you and is distressed because you heard he was ill. Indeed, he was ill and almost died. But God had mercy on him, and not on him only but also on me, to spare me sorrow upon sorrow. Philippians 2:23-27

Epaphroditus was a representative from the church in Philippi, sent by the church to Rome to comfort and encourage Paul. Now Paul is releasing him to return home.

Do you have people you support, comfort or mentor? Pray for them today.

Prayer: Dear Heavenly Father, Thank you for those people who have been in my life *(name them here)* to help me grow through discipleship and mentoring. May I be in their place for someone else? Amen.

Journal

____

____

____

____

____

Day 173

Therefore, I am more eager to send him, so that when you see him again you may be glad and I may have less anxiety. So then, welcome him in the Lord with great joy, and honor people like him, because he almost died for the work of Christ. He risked his life to make up for the help you yourselves could not give me. Philippians 2:28-30

We can see the humanity in Paul as he commends both Timothy and Epaphroditus in this section of verses. His care for his personal friends and the church in Philippi is evident in his letter.

How do you care for your friends? Do you keep in touch with them via text, email, phone calls, coffee/lunch, or ......? Do you encourage, support and pray for your family, friends, acquaintances and people you see or meet? Journal your responses.

Prayer: Dear Heavenly Father, I pray for *(mention your family, friends, acquaintances)*, asking you to watch over them and lead them into all righteousness. Place on my heart who I should reach out to, and when, so I may encourage them in you. Amen.

Journal

Day 174

Further, my brothers and sisters, rejoice in the Lord! It is no trouble for me to write the same things to you again, and it is a safeguard for you. Philippians 3:1

Perhaps Paul had dealt with the upcoming concern either orally or in another letter. Whatever way, he is to repeat himself again as a 'safeguard' to his beloved church.

We also need truths to be repeated to us for our understanding.

Prayer: Dear Heavenly Father, Thank you for your faithfulness to me and not giving up on me when the road was tough and I needed extra guidance and care. Amen.

Journal

____
____
____
____
____

Day 175

Watch out for those dogs, those evildoers, those mutilators of the flesh. For it is we who are the circumcision, we who serve God by his Spirit, who boast in Christ Jesus, and who put no confidence in the flesh - though I myself have reasons for such confidence. Philippians 3:2-4a

True circumcision, as Paul refers to here, is when believers, who worship God with genuine spiritual worship, and who glory in Christ as their Savior rather than trusting in their own human effort. It is circumcision of the heart. Paul's warning the church at Philippi to watch out for the false teaching of the Judiazers. In our day, also, it is easy to get caught up in false teaching - as there is much around. Keep safe by bathing yourself in prayer, Bible Study and Christian fellowship.

Prayer: Dear Heavenly Father, keep me from veering off the path you have set for me, and keep me true to your word. Amen

Journal

____

____

____

____

____

Day 176

"If someone else thinks they have reasons to put confidence in the flesh, I have more: circumcised on the eighth day, of the people of Israel, of the tribe of Benjamin, Hebrew of Hebrews; in regard to the law, a Pharisee; as for zeal, persecuting the church; as for righteousness based on the law, faultless. Philippians 3:4b-6

Here Paul describes his pre christian experience, and his pious religiousness. He was totally committed to the ways and traditions of the Pharisees. He uses this description to explain to his readers that he fully understands Judiasm, in order to refute the Judiazers. Incidentally, once he met Jesus, he was totally committed to the ways of Jesus.

Prayer: Dear Heavenly Father, Help me to be zealous for you in my christian walk. May I be like you and be totally sold out for the Kingdom of God, and its purpose in human history. Amen.

Journal

____

____

____

____

____

Day 177

But whatever were gains to me I now consider loss for the sake of Christ. What is more, I consider everything a loss because of the surpassing worth of knowing Christ Jesus my Lord, for whose sake I have lost all things. I consider them garbage, that I may gain Christ and be found in him, not having a righteousness of my own that comes from the law, but that which is through faith in Christ - the righteousness that comes from God on the basis of faith. Philippians 3:7-9

Pauls reversal began on the road to Damascus, where he personally met Jesus. The reversal was from being self-centered, to becoming centered in Christ. He experienced that life giving transformation that comes from knowing Christ Jesus.

Journal transformations you have observed in your life of following Christ Jesus.

Prayer: Dear Heavenly Father, thank you for your transformation power in my life. I choose to allow the Holy Spirit into my being to work the good work of making or transforming me to be more like you. Help me to be brave when I am confronted with things which are hard to bear, I know you are always near and you hold my hand. Amen.

Journal

____

____

____

____

____

Day 178

I want to know Christ - yes, to know the power of his resurrection and participation in his sufferings, becoming like him in his death, and so, somehow to attain to the resurrection of the dead. Philippians 3:10,11

Paul is stating his desire to know Christ in its fullest meaning. He states that his desire is to share Christ's sufferings and death. Such deep love he had for the Lord.

How well do you know Jesus? Have you let him become Lord of your life? What does that mean to you? Journal your thoughts.

Prayer: Dear Heavenly Father, I love you Lord, your mercies in my life are never ending. All my life you have been and still faithful to me, you have been so good to me.

I praise you and am thankful for your goodness to me. Amen.

Journal

____

____

____

____

____

Day 179

Not that I have already obtained all this, or have already arrived at my goal, but I press on to take hold of that for which Christ Jesus took hold of me. Philippians 3:12

Paul's goal was the goal which Christ Jesus had for him. The best part is that Christ Jesus supplied the resources for him to press on toward the goal, as he does for us. Paul wanted everything the Lord desired for him, even if it did mean a Roman prison. After all, his mind and his love for Jesus and humanity were not imprisoned while there, it was only his body.

How do you fare in difficult circumstances? Do you call out to Jesus for comfort, support and guidance? Do you include others in your life? Do you become inward looking and depressed, or, outward looking to trust and praise God?

Prayer: Dear Heavenly Father, help me when times are tough. I want to see you through the difficulties and focus on you and not the surrounding events or feelings. I ask that you give me faith and strength, so I may reach out to you, and hold your hand. Thank you for your promise to be with me at all times. Amen.

Journal

____

____

____

____

____

Day 180

Brothers and sisters, I do not consider myself yet to have taken hold of it. But one thing I do; Forgetting what is behind and straining toward what is ahead, I press on toward the goal to win the prize for which God has called me heavenward in Christ Jesus. Philippians 3:13,14

Paul is suggesting that his past is dealt with and forgiven so he has set his mind and actions on a life which leads to the award of everlasting life in heaven with Jesus.

Do you live each day with the focus of living for Jesus, in all you do, think and say? Journal your thoughts.

Prayer: Dear Heavenly Father, I want to press on toward what is ahead and forget what is behind. I want all that you have planned for me in the name of Jesus. Amen.

Journal

____

____

____

____

____

Day 181

All of us, then, who are mature should take such a view of things. And if on some point you think differently, that too God will make clear to you. Only let us live up to what we have already attained. Philippians 3:15,16

Here Paul is asking us to live up to the truth about Jesus. His overwhelming, unconditional love towards us, his redemption plan which he worked out for us, his loving and trustworthy promises he has made for us to be successful, his word and all the instruction it contains.

Oh, how he loves you and me. He gave his son (Jesus), what more could he give?

Prayer: Dear Heavenly Father, Thank you for your redemption plan and your willingness to be abused and maligned for me. Thank you for your lavish love poured on me through the redemption plan. Thank you for freeing me from my old life and making me new. I love you. Amen.

Journal

____

____

____

____

____

Day 182

Join together in following my example, brothers and sisters, and just as you have us as a model, keep your eyes on those who live as we do. For, as I have often told you before and now tell you again even with tears, many live as enemies of the cross of Christ. Philippians 3:17,18

So, it is today, there are many enemies of the Cross of Christ. Political regimes seek out and kill Christians. Certain religions excommunicate families or family members from their community, should they convert to Christianity.

Today, pray for and seek organizations who help the persecuted church and its members. Become engaged in your support of the community of believers.

Prayer: Dear Heavenly Father, guide me to people and places and organizations where I can pray and support the work they do in helping persecuted christians, and, other persecuted groups. Amen.

Journal

____

____

____

____

Day 183

Their destiny is destruction, their god is their stomach and their glory is in their shame. Their mind is on earthly things. But our citizenship is in heaven. And we eagerly await a Savior from there, the Lord Jesus Christ, who, by the power that enables him to bring everything under his control, will transform our lowly bodies, so they will be like his glorious body. Philippians 3:19-21

Paul describes, somewhat, the eventuality of the enemies of the Cross of Christ, and compares it with the prize for those who follow Christ. Christ's power comes from his exalted position due to his obedience to the cross and his resurrection. Christians will receive theirs on their salvation and death, or, when Christ comes again, if we are still alive whichever comes first.

Prayer: Dear Heavenly Father, Thank you for your promise of eternal life with you in your home. I am excited to live with you eternally. Help me, in the meantime, to be found doing your work here on earth as you have asked me - being a light on a hill, the salt of the earth, sowing seeds of righteousness, leading others to you, discipling and mentoring folk and letting you transform me into your likeness. Amen.

Journal

____

____

____

____

____

Day 184

Therefore, my brothers and sisters, you whom I love and long for, my joy and crown, stand firm in the Lord in this way, dear friends! Philippians 4:1

Have you noticed and enjoyed reading about and learning from the love Paul has for the church in Philippi? How does it compare with your place of worship? How does it compare with the relationships in your life?

Today, Journal praises about your place of worship and relationships, and prayers or needs you have in those areas.

Prayer: Dear Heavenly Father, I praise you for my place of fellowship *(name the church)* and those who are in my spiritual family. Thank you for placing them in my life to 'do life together'. I pray for provision for *(name the needs of those in your church, and needs of the church)* and thank you for the answers you provide. Amen.

Journal

____

____

____

____

____

Day 185

I plead with Euodia and I plead with Synthyche to be of the same mind in the Lord. Yes, I ask you, my true companion, help these women since they have contended at my side in the cause of the gospel, along with Clement and the rest of my co-workers, whose names are in the book of life. Philippians 4:2,3

We see how personable Paul is with his friends, here in this passage, writing from imprisonment in Rome he is still aware of and loving on these friends even though some are quarreling.

Are we like that with our friends, still interested in them even though they are out of sight? Think of people in your life and pray a blessing on each one of them. Praise God for his purpose in their lives.

Prayer: Dear Heavenly Father, thank you for friends in my life. I thank you for *(name friends)*. I appreciate them and ask you to bless them for their goodness and kindness to me. May I be a good friend to them. Amen.

Journal

____
____
____
____
____

Day 186

Rejoice in the Lord always, I will say it again, Rejoice! Let your gentleness be evident to all. The Lord is near. Philippians 4:4,5

We are to rejoice, no matter what. Should things be going well, or not so well, we are to rejoice. Think about what that says to those around us who are non-believers, especially when gentleness is added into the mix. The Lord's second coming is near - this is the next great event in the calendar of the church.

Are you ready for him to return at any time, in your day or night? How will he find you?

Prayer: Dear Heavenly Father, I rejoice in you for many things, but most of all, I rejoice that you are in my heart and in my life. I will rejoice wholeheartedly when you come to take me home. Amen.

Journal

____

____

____

____

____

Day 187

Do not be anxious about anything, but in every situation, by prayer and petition, with thanksgiving, present your requests to God. Philippians 4:6

This verse tells us to replace our anxiety with thanksgiving. It means for you to thankfully present your prayers to God, for the item or situation which you are making the petition about. This runs opposite to our natural desires since we would normally fret or complain. Our Lord wants our heart to change and for us to thank him for what comes our way. Who knows, it might be a growth test.

Today, pray to the Lord and present your petitions to him in a thankful manner.

Prayer: Dear Heavenly Father, I thankfully present my petitions to you. Thank you for *(name your petitions or worries)* in my life so that I can trust you more and excitedly see your hand of grace in each of them. Amen.

Journal

____

____

____

____

Day 188

And the peace of God which transcends all understanding, will guard your hearts and minds in Christ Jesus. Philippians 4:7

This peace is an inner tranquility based on faith, trust and stillness with God - the peaceful state of those whose sins are forgiven. On the scale of 0 being low and 10 being high, where do you measure on the peace scale in your life?

Talk to the Lord about your anxieties, lay them at his feet. Listen to and sing the song 'He is my peace, he has broken down every chain'.

Prayer: Dear Heavenly Father, thank you for your peace which is offered to me. Thank you, I can come to you and rest in your arms and be calm and safe. Thank you for the stillness you give to us in your presence. I love you. Amen.

Journal

____

____

____

____

____

Day 189

Finally, brothers and sisters, whatever is true, whatever is noble, whatever is right, whatever is pure, whatever is lovely, whatever is admirable - if anything is excellent or praiseworthy - think about such things. Philippians 4:8

These thought patterns are sure to produce a wholesome individual. Our thoughts influence our speech and actions, which ultimately influence our life choices. May we be found as one who thinks wholesome thoughts and speaks words of hope and healing.

Prayer: Dear Heavenly Father, I pray that my mind will think on things that are true, noble, right, pure, things that are lovely and admirable. Keep my mind and thoughts on the positives and keep me connected to you. Amen.

Journal

____
____
____
____
____

Day 190

Whatever you have learned or received, or heard from me, or seen in me - put it into practice. And the God of peace will be with you. I rejoiced greatly in the Lord that at last you have renewed your concern for me. Indeed, you have been concerned but you had no opportunity to show it. Philippians 4:9,10

In those days there was no internet or motor vehicles. Messages were sent by horse or foot - therefore there were delays in sending messages or receiving a response. In this passage, there are all sorts of hypothesis as to what Paul was meaning.

How do you feel when you don't get responses, or your messages don't get through to the person(s) they were meant for? Journal your memories, feelings and thoughts.

Prayer: Dear Heavenly Father, thank you for the technology and connectedness we have today. Yes, it can be a blessing and a curse, but thank you when it works well because we can keep in touch with our friends and family. Amen.

Journal

____

____

____

____

____

Day 191

I am not saying this because I am in need, for I have learned to be content whatever the circumstances. I know what it is to be in need, for I have learned to be content whatever the circumstances. I know what it is to be in need, and I know what it is to have plenty or in want. Philippians 4:11,12

Again, on the scale of 1-10, how is your contentment level? Are you trusting our Lord to provide for you? What are you praying for? Is it a spouse, a family, a job, good grades, a happy home......you fill in the blanks.

Prayer: Dear Heavenly Father, help me to be contend in you. Help me to rely more fully on you. Help me to live a life with less of me and more of you, and to purposefully rely on you. I trust you. Amen.

Journal

____

____

____

____

____

Day 192

I can do everything through him who gives me strength. Philippians 4:13

Being at one with Jesus Christ is the secret of being content, and the source of Paul's abiding strength. He is also the source of our abiding strength. He is the one we run to and hide. He is the one who carries us when we are afraid. He is the one who loves us unconditionally and redeemed us from sin. He is the one who has adopted us into his family. He is the one, the only living and exalted Jesus Christ our Lord.

Prayer: Dear Heavenly Father, Oh how I love you. Only you are my strength and song. You life me up when I fall down, you walk beside me as we travel through the valley of death, you restore me. I humbly bow before you in gratitude and love. Amen.

Journal

____

____

____

____

____

Day 193

Yet it was good of you to share in my troubles. Moreover, as you Philippians know, in the early days of your acquaintance with the gospel, when I set out from Macedonia, not one church shared with me in the manner of giving and receiving, except you only, for even when I was in Thessolinica, you sent me aid more than once when I was in need. Philippians 4:14-16

Paul acknowledges and commends the church at Philippi for their faithful giving to him and receiving from him, even while he was a prisoner in Rome.

This brings up the subject of our giving. What does this passage speak to you. A tithe is 10% of an income, and offerings are over and above a tithe. Ask the Lord to speak to you about your tithes and offerings.

Prayer: Dear Heavenly Father, Thank you for the financial income you give to me. Help me to be honest and caring to return my tithe to you. Give me a generous spirit so I can be a conduit whom you give to others through. Amen.

Journal

____

____

____

____

____

Day 194

Not that I desire your gifts; what I desire more is that more be credited to your account. I have received full payment and have more than enough; I am amply supplied, now that I have received from Epaphroditus the gifts you sent. They are a fragrant offering, an acceptable sacrifice pleasing to God. Philippians 4:17,18

I love the phrase 'they are a fragrant offering, an acceptable sacrifice, pleasing to God'. What does that phrase mean to you? Journal your thoughts. Your gifts and offerings doesn't have to be only money, they could be your time, your skill, your love, food parcels, reaching out to those in need.

Prayer: Dear Heavenly Father, I give myself to you as a living sacrifice. I give to you my time, skill, love, willing heart to reach out to those in need. Open my eyes and ears to see and hear of those who are in need of the talents which you have give to me, so that I may share them in your name. Amen.

Journal

____

____

____

____

____

Day 195

And my God will meet all your needs according to the riches of his glory in Christ Jesus. To our God and Father be glory forever and ever, Amen. Greet all God's people in Christ Jesus. The brothers and sisters who are with me send greetings. All the God's people here send you greetings, especially those who belong to Caesar's household. The grace of the Lord Jesus Christ be with your spirit. Amen. Philippians 4:19-23

Our Lord's promise is to forever look after your needs. He is well able to care for you, though it may not be in a way we expect as he is in the 'moulding' business, moulding you to be more like him.

Listen to the song - "He owns the cattle on a thousand hills, the wealth in every mine. He owns the rivers, the rocks and hills, the sun, the stars that shine."

Prayer: Dear Heavenly Father, Thank you for your abundant provision given to me. Thank you for caring for my needs. Please use me to help provide for the needs of those around me. Amen.

Journal

____

____

____

____

Day 196

Paul an apostle of Christ Jesus by the will of God, and Timothy our brother. To

God's holy people in Colossae. Grace and Peace to you from God our Father. Colossians 1:1,2

The letter to the saints in Colossae, begins with Paul identifying himself, along with his credentials and his friend, Timothy. He wrote this letter to the church in Colossae to refute the invasion of the heresy of Gnosticism. We will see how Paul proclaims Jesus as being completely God and completely man - the fullness of the deity in the form of man. Jesus is completely adequate for his mission of salvation, whereas, Gnosticism was completely inadequate. Gnosticism claimed that salvation could be gained through a special form of secret knowledge.

Prayer: Dear Heavenly Father, Thank you that it is you who is the light of the world, it is you to whom we run, the Holy Bible is your Word, and your Word it truth. Amen.

Journal

Day 197

We always thank God, the Father of our Lord Jesus Christ, when we pray for you, because we have heard of your faith in Christ Jesus and of the love you have for all God's people,…. Colossians 1:3,4

Paul's example to us is to pray for fellow saints, or Christians, and to prayerfully thank the Lord for each other. This creates unity, teamwork, joy, and pleasantness. How do you see those with whom you worship? Are they your prayer projects, friends, team workers? Pray for those who come to mind today.

Prayer: Dear Heavenly Father, I pray for *(who comes to mind)* and ask that you bless them with abundant joy and peace today. Thank you for arranging our lives so that we are family together. Amen.

Journal

____

____

____

____

____

Day 198

...the faith and love that spring from the hope stored up for you in heaven and about which you have already heard in the true message of the gospel that has come to you. In the same way the gospel is bearing fruit and growing throughout the whole world - just as it has been doing among you since the day you heard it and truly understood God's grace. Colossians 1:5,6

All over the world - means the rapid spread of the gospel into every quarter of the Roman Empire within three decades of Pentecost. Nowadays we know as worldwide evangelism. Jesus asked us to 'Go and make disciples of all nations, baptizing them in the name of the Father and of the Son and of the Holy Spirit, and teaching them to obey everything I have commanded you. Matthew 28:21,22b. There is more to do, but praise God the wonderful message of the Gospel is has spread and is spreading.

Prayer: Dear Heavenly Father, I pray for worldwide evangelism, especially in the countries where their culture is anti-Christian, such as Communist countries, Hindu countries and Islamic countries. Break down the doors of deception over those places and in the hearts of their people with you precious love and salvation offered to them, and free them to be able to hear your voice. Amen.

Journal

____

____

____

____

____

Day 199

You learned it from Ephaphras, our dear fellow servant, who is a faithful minister of Christ on our behalf, and who told us of your love in the Spirit. For this reason, since the day we heard about you, we have not stopped praying for you. We continually ask God to fill you with the knowledge of his will, through all wisdom and understanding that the Spirit gives,...
Colossians 1:7-9

Again, we see Paul talking about praying for each other. This is a wonderful example to us to follow his leading and pray for each other, the worldwide and local church, our town, country, current events, joys, sorrows and more. Make a list.

Prayer: Dear Heavenly Father, I bring to you *(name the items on your list)* and pray for each. I pray for truth to be upheld, for your guidance of our leaders - both civic and spiritual, for peace and joy. I bring to you *(name certain events or situations)* and ask for you to place your hand on them and have your way. Amen.

Journal

Day 200

...so that you may live a life worthy of the Lord and may please him in every way: bearing fruit in every good work, growing in the knowledge of God, being strengthened with all power according to his glorious might so that you may have great endurance and patience, and giving joyful thanks to the Father who has qualified you to share in the inheritance of his holy people in the kingdom of light. Colossians 1:10-12

The church at Colossae were uplifted in prayer by Paul and his fellow Christians, that they would be strong, strengthened b the power of God, to grow in the knowledge of Christ Jesus and live in the light of the Gospel. Does this prayer uplift you?

Prayer: Dear Heavenly Father, I want to please you in every way, to bear fruit in good work and to grow in knowledge of you. I want to be strengthened with your power so I will have endurance, patience and joy. Thank you for loving me. Amen.

Journal

____

____

____

____

____

Day 201

For he has rescued us from the dominion of darkness and brought us into the kingdom of the Son he loves, in whom we have redemption, the forgiveness of sins. Colossians 1:13,14

Christians now live in the benevolent rule of Christ Jesus our Savior. Our Savior paid the price for our sins and we are clean in his sight, by his blood we are forgiven of all our infractions. The Lord's prayer (Matthew 6:12) states, 'Forgive our debts as we forgive our debtors.' Forgiveness is to be passed on to others. Forgiveness is very healing.

Prayer: Dear Heavenly Father, I know you want me to forgive others. I know it is a choice and I choose forgiveness for infringements others have done to me. I forgive *(name the person)*. Help me to forgive in the same manner in which you forgave me. Teach me to forgive and forget. Amen.

Journal

____

____

____

____

____

Day 202

The Son is the image of the invisible God, the firstborn over all creation. For in him all things were created: things in heaven and on earth, visible and invisible, whether thrones or powers or rulers or authorities; all things have been created through him and for him. Colossians 1:15,16

Christ is the exact representation of God's being - see Hebrews 1:3 as it says the same thing. He represents God on earth as the firstborn and has all the privileges of a firstborn - inheritance and rights. Christ is the firstborn since he is the first and only human to have been resurrected from death to life, and he continues to live forevermore. Whereas, others who have been raised from the dead, died again later.

Prayer: Dear Heavenly Father, I honor and worship you, my Lord and my God. You are my King of Kings and my Lord of Lords. You are my Savior, Redeemer, my Refuge and strong fortress to whom I run to. I trust you, love you, honor you and worship you. Amen.

Journal

____

____

____

____

Day 203

He is before all things and in him all things hold together. And he is the head of the body, the church, he is the beginning and the firstborn from among the dead, so that in everything he might have the supremacy. Colossians 1:17,18

Christ is the supreme head of the body of Christ, which is the church. It is he to whom we pray, worship, praise and adore, not to Mary nor the saints. Even though Mary and the saints were wonderful examples to follow, it is Jesus who is the savior, and the mediator between God and Man. It was Jesus who is the Son of God who died for our sins, and was raised up to life again. He is the supreme head of the body of Christ. See 1 Timothy 2:5. Praise, worship and petition our supreme Christ, the head of the Church.

Prayer: Dear Heavenly Father, Thank you that it is Jesus who is the supreme head of your body. It is he who was tortured, murdered and rose again for the redemption of the human race, nothing or no-one else. Praise God and Hallelujah. Amen.

Journal

____

____

____

____

____

Day 204

For God was pleased to have all his fullness dwell in him, and through him to reconcile to himself all things, whether things on earth or things in heaven, by making peace, through his blood, shed on the cross. Colossians 1:19,20

'Fulness' here means the total and complete powers of God.

Reconciliation with Christ comes at conversion, which is offered to everyone. Reconciliation of nature comes at the return of Christ - Romans 8:21. God pleases to live in you - he knows you by name, he has a perfect plan for your life. How do you respond?

Prayer: Dear Heavenly Father, Thank you for including me in your plan of salvation. I accepted you when you first approached me, and I still accept and want you to live inside of me. I want your perfect plan to be worked out in my life. I want you. Thank you for your love for men. Amen.

Journal

____

____

____

____

____

Day 205

Once you were alienated from God and were enemies in your minds because of your evil behavior. But now he has reconciled you by Christ's physical body through death to present you holy in his sight, without blemish and free of accusation,... Colossians 1:21,22

God's saving grace and his perfect plan of redemption has taken us from foe to friend in God's company. Christ's obedience and fulfillment of the redemptive plan gives us access to our Holy God, on condition that we accept Christ's sacrifice for us and receive forgiveness for our sin, which is washed in Chris's blood. Hallelujah - I accept.

Today sing the old hymn, What can wash away my sin, nothing but the blood of Jesus.

Journal

____

____

____

____

____

Day 206

...if you continue in your faith, established and firm, and do not move from the hope held out in the gospel. This is the gospel that you heard and that has been proclaimed to every creature under heaven, and of which I, Paul, have become a servant. Colossians 1:23

Continuing on from v22, we are presented to God holy and unblemished if we continue in our faith. Christ offers hope. The gospel offers hope. Praise God for the Gospel. The meaning of the gospel is 'good news' An acronym for the gospel is God Offers Sinful People Eternal Life. The gospel is our freedom from sin, through Jesus Christ.

Prayer: Dear Heavenly Father, thank you for offering sinful me eternal life. Thank you, I accepted it. Help me to grow to be more like you. Help me to be aware of situations when you want me to share my 'God Story' to others. Amen.

Journal

____

____

____

____

____

Day 207

Now I rejoice in what I am suffering for you, and I fill up in my flesh what is still lacking in regards to Christ's afflictions, for the sake of his body, which is the church. I have become its servant by the commission God gave me to present to you the word of God and its fullness - the mystery that has been kept hidden for ages and generations but is now disclosed to the Lord's people. Colossians 1:24-26

The Christian mystery is not secret knowledge for just a few of us. It is a revelation of divine truths - once hidden before Christ, but now openly proclaimed after Christ. Remember Matthew 28:20? Jesus commissions us to take the gospel to all nations - to every tongue and people. Praise God for his grace to open to you and me the truth of salvation, redemption and evangelism.

Prayer: Dear Heavenly Father, your love is all encompassing and for all the human race, not just a select few. Amen.

Journal

____

____

____

____

____

Day 208

To them God has chosen to make known among the Gentiles the glorious riches of this mystery, which is Christ in you, the hope of glory. Colossians 1:27

The wonderful mystery which Paul mentions is that the gospel of Christ is available for Jews and Gentiles, and that being so, it is on the same terms for both Jews and Gentiles. God has chosen us, the gentile community to have equal terms with the people of promise, the Jews. This is through Christ Jesus. In context, this was an amazing but difficult revelation to the Jews. Praise God for his unfailing promises to you and me.

Prayer: Dear Heavenly Father, Hallelujah for the Lord my God, the Almighty reigns. I will rejoice and be glad, and give all glory unto him. Amen.

Journal

____

____

____

____

____

Day 209

He is the one we proclaim, admonishing and teaching everyone with all wisdom, so that we may present everyone fully mature in Christ. To this end I strenuously contend, with all the energy Christ so powerfully works in me. Colossians 1:28,29

Paul's mission is evangelism and discipleship, to present us to the Lord fully mature. There is no secrecy or special knowledge which the gnostics proclaimed, we are each equally and fully informed of the Cross of Christ, forgiveness of sins, and the redemptive power of Christ's blood, which is freely available to everyone, no matter who we are. Praise God for his love to humanity - to you and me personally.

Prayer: Dear Heavenly Father, I love you Lord for your mercy reigns forever, all my days will I seek to serve and love you. For you are Supreme, regal, loving, kind and truthful, and I will sing of your faithfulness to me forever. Amen,

Journal

____

____

____

____

____

Day 210

I want you to know how much I am contending for you and for those at Laodicia, and for all those who have not met me personally. My goal is that they may be encouraged in heart and united in love, so that they may have the full riches of complete understanding, in order that they may know the mystery of God, namely Christ, in whom are hidden all the treasures of wisdom and knowledge. Colossians 2:1-3

We see that Paul stressed knowing fullness of the riches of complete understanding and knowledge in this letter - because he was refuting a heresy which emphasized knowledge as the means of Salvation, i.e., -gnosticism. Praise God, with Christ he has given us, his church, the treasures of wisdom and knowledge and we don't have to make any new ideology us, because we are complete in him.

Prayer: Dear Heavenly Father, Jesus is our all in all. He is the perfect Savior, the Son of Man without sin, who knows what it is to be a human, and who stands as a mediator between you and me. You sent him as the perfect and unblemished sacrifice for my sins. You are Perfect in every way. Thank you for your faithfulness and your trustworthiness. I love you. Amen.

Journal

____

____

____

____

____

Day 211

I tell you this so that no one may deceive you by fine sounding arguments. For though I am absent from you in the body, I am present with you in spirit and delight to see how disciplined you are and how firm your faith in Christ is. Colossians 2:4,5

Kind, caring words from a man who cares for the sincerity and wellbeing of a fledgling church under heretical attack. At this point, go ahead and check your sincerity toward others who are not in your presence. How do you love on them from afar? Journal your responses.

Prayer: Dear Heavenly Father, I think of *(name those who are afar)* and ask for you to bless them with kindness, peace and Joy. Remind me to reach out to them with kind and caring words. Amen.

Journal

____

____

____

____

Day 212

So then, just as you received Christ Jesus as Lord, continue to live your lives in him, 'rooted' and built up in him, strengthened in the faith as you were taught, and overflowing with thankfulness. 1 Colossians 2:6

Paul urges the church in Colossae, and us, to continue to live a life with which the foundation is rooted, built and strengthened in Christ Jesus. It is by faith that we are to take our daily steps within the life Christ has given us to live.

Prayer: Dear Heavenly Father, Walk with me today. Help me with my attitudes. Let my speech be wholesome, kind and truthful. May I be your eyes, ears, hands and feet to reach someone for you today. Amen.

Journal

____

____

____

____

____

Day 213

See to it that no one takes you captive through hollow and deceptive philosophy, which depends on human tradition and the elemental spiritual forces of this world rather than on Christ. For in Christ all the fullness of the Deity lives in bodily form, and in Christ you have been brought to fullness. He is the head over every power and authority. Colossians 2:7-10

These verses describe our completeness in Christ. He is everything we need. Paul uses these verses to dispel the philosophy of the gnostics who claim Christ is deficient. Jesus is God, he is their God and is our God, he never changes, his love for you and me remains full and complete. He was, is and is to come. He is never ending and always true.

Prayer: Dear Heavenly Father, Oh how we can trust you. Your love and goodness is lavishly overflowing towards me. I have comfort in knowing you are true and real. Keep my eyes on you and my ears hearing your still sweet voice speaking to me. Amen.

Journal

____
____
____
____
____

Day 214

In him you were also circumcised with a circumcision not performed by human hands. Your whole self-ruled by the flesh was put off when you were circumcised by Christ, having been buried with him in baptism, in which you were raised with him through your faith in the working of God, who raised him from the dead. Colossians 2:11,12

Some commentaries suggest that while this is the only reference where circumcision is associated with baptism, some see the passage as implying that, for the Christian, water baptism is a sign of covenant relationship. Noting, also, in the Jewish faith, circumcision is a sign of covenant relationship.

Prayer: Dear Heavenly Father, I love you Lord and I lift my voice, to worship you, Oh my God. Rejoice my King in what you hear, let me be a sweet sound in your ear. Amen.

Journal

____

____

____

____

____

Day 215

When you were dead in your sins and in the uncircumcision of your flesh, God made you alive with Christ. He forgave us all our sins, having canceled the charge of our legal indebtedness, which stood against us and condemned us; he has taken it away, by nailing it to the cross. Colossians 2:13,14

Here Paul is referring to the Jewish laws as the 'written code'. Nobody was able to follow those laws, that is why all those Old Testament sacrifices were needed to atone for people, or make them at one with God. Jesus became the sacrifice, once and for all, and has given those who believe, freedom from the debt of sin, and power to live as an overcomer.

Prayer: Dear Heavenly Father, Oh my Lord, what a Savior. A Savior who volunteered to be tortured and murdered on a Roman cross, die and rise again three days later. What can I say? I cannot say anything other than get on my knees, raise my hands to you and proclaim Hallelujah! Amen.

Journal

____

____

____

____

____

Day 216

And having disarmed the powers and authorities he made a public spectacle of them triumphing over them by the cross! Colossians 2:15

Wow! Not only did God cancel out the accusations of the law or sin, but he also conquered and disarmed the evil angels who entice people to follow themselves, schisms and false teachings about Christ. This is a powerful verse, laying out the incredible effect of Christ's sacrifice on the cross, and the freedom which he offers his followers. Today, raise your arms and bow your knees to the most powerful God, Jesus Christ, and love on him.

Prayer: Dear Heavenly Father, Oh my Lord, what a Savior. A Savior who volunteered to be tortured and murdered on a Roman cross, die and rise again three days later. What can I say? I cannot say anything other than get on my knees, raise my hands to you and proclaim Hallelujah! Amen.

Journal

____

____

____

____

____

Day 217

Therefore, do not let anyone judge you by what you eat or drink, or with regard to a religious festival, a new moon celebration or a Sabbath day. These are a shadow of the things that were to come; the reality, however, is found in Christ. Colossians 2:16,17

The festivals, food regulations etc were symbolic of the old covenant. However, since the Messiah has been revealed, and established the new covenant, there is not a need to pursue them. In essence, Paul continues to refute the Colossian heresay.

Prayer: Dear Heavenly Father, Thank you that you have made me complete in you. I do not need to do anything other than open my heart to you, let you live in me and transform me into the person you designed me to be. Amen.

Journal

____

____

____

____

____

Day 218

Do not let anyone who delights in false humility and the worship of angels disqualify you. Such a person goes into great detail about what he has seen; they are puffed up with idle notions by their unspiritual mind. They have lost connection with the head, from whom the whole body is supported and held together by its ligaments and sinews, grows as God causes it to grow.
Colossians 2:18,19

Paul again is refuting the worship of angels or spirit beings which the gnostics follow. He is advising that following this heresy will 'disqualify them from the prize'. The 'prize' is Christ Jesus in all his fullness, power, beauty and truth.

Prayer: Dear Heavenly Father, I want to run the race with you and win the prize which is you. Thank you for reaching out to me, loving on me, saving me, and keeping me in your will. Amen.

Journal

____

____

____

____

____

Day 219

Since you died with Christ to the elemental spiritual forces of this world, why, as though you still belong to it, do you submit to its rules? Do not handle! Do not taste! Do not touch! These rules, which have to do with things that are all destined to perish with use, are based on merely human commands and teachings. Such regulations indeed have the appearance of wisdom, with their self-imposed worship, their false humility, and their harsh treatment of the body, but they lack any value in restraining sensual indulgence. Colossians 2:20-23

We do not need to follow legal rules to reach Jesus. He has offered us grace as a free and unmerited gift. Salvation is free, by faith, and not by works, lest any person boast about it. So, there is no expectations of any ritual or indoctrination experience. Jesus wants our heart, and he wants us to give it to him by choice. Praise God for his love for his body, which he does not punish. He loves his body, the church, which is you and me.

Prayer: Dear Heavenly Father, Thank you for your free gift of salvation which is given to us by faith and not by works. Thank you for your foresight, you know how humans work, so you made it easy for us to have access to you - freely. What an amazing and awesome God you are. Amen.

Journal

____

____

____

____

____

Day 220

Since then, you have been raised with Christ, set your hearts on things above, where Christ is seated at the right hand of God. Set your mind on things above, not on earthly things. Colossians 3:1,2

We are <u>in</u> the world but not <u>of</u> it - just a-passin-through! Our old self is meant to be crucified with Christ. For example, putting off envy, hate, unrighteous anger etc, and, pursuing caring for our neighbor, living for Jesus and not ourselves, living a righteous life, i.e., standing up for what is right, serving, living honestly, putting others ahead of ourselves, and so on. Today Journal ways you 'set your mind on things above'.

Prayer: Dear Heavenly Father, Help me to put on my new self and set my mind on things that please you. Help me to rest in you as you work the transforming work in my mind. Keep my eyes and ears on you. Amen.

Journal

____

____

____

____

____

Day 221

For you died and your life is now hidden with Christ in God. When Christ, who is your life, appears, then you also will appear with him in Glory. Colossians 3:3,4

When we accepted the truth of Christ Jesus and asked him into our life and world, we died to our old life. Baptism is a picture of dying to the old life and being raised to a new life. We are continually being transformed by the renewing of our mind, by our wonderful Lord - see Romans 12:2, Philippians 2:12. We are taken into God's tender care as he guides us into all truth. Praise him for his tender love and care toward you, he rescued you and is growing you to be more like him. You are a blessing to him and the 'apple of his eye', Psalm 17:8, Proverbs 7:2

Prayer: Dear Heavenly Father, I praise you for your tender love and care toward me. Thank you for rescuing me and growing me to become more like you. I love you and I love your presence with me. Amen.

Journal

____

____

____

____

____

Day 222

Put to death, therefore, whatever belongs to your earthly nature: sexual immorality, impurity, lust, evil desires and greed, which is idolatry. Because of these, the wrath of God is coming. You used to walk in these ways, in the life you once lived. But now you must also rid yourselves of all such things as these: anger, rage, malice, slander and filthy language from your lips. Colossians 3:5-8

God is opposed to sin, this is why Paul lists out the offenses, so we may check in with ourselves and do a soul search to repent of any sin which may be lingering within us.

Prayer: Dear Heavenly Father, I ask you to search my heart again. Check my motives, thoughts and dreams, that I may honor you in all things. Help me to hear your prompting. Amen.

Journal

____

____

____

____

____

Day 223

Do not lie to each other, since you have taken off your old self with its practices, and put on the new self, which is being renewed in knowledge in the image of its Creator. Here there is no Gentile or Jew, circumcised or uncircumcised, barbarian, Scythian, slave or free, but Christ is all, and is in all. Colossians 3:9-11

When we put off the old self, it is an imagery of getting rid of our old, sinful ways. Putting on the new self reflects stepping into a new life with Christ as our goal. In God's sight, all humans are the same, no matter which category we are defined on earth. Praise God he is not a racist! He loves each of us, warts and all!!!!

Prayer: Dear Heavenly Father, You know all generations, languages and nations. Nothing is a surprise to you, not the way we look, the way we speak, what we eat or our daily habits. You know all of us and love on each of us, no matter what. Thank you for your all-encompassing love. Amen.

Journal

____

____

____

____

____

Day 224

Therefore, as God's chosen people, <u>holy and dearly loved,</u> clothe yourselves with compassion, kindness, humility, gentleness and patience. Bear with each other and forgive one another if any of you has a grievance against someone. Colossians 12,13a

As a human you are dearly loved. As a Christian, you are dearly loved and considered to be one of God's chosen people - he has adopted you into his family. Ephesians 1:15. Paul has listed attributes with which we should emanate, as we are instructed to wear them. How are you managing compassion, kindness, humility, gentleness and patience in your life. Journal your responses and pray the prayer, 'Lord, more of you and less of me.'

Prayer: Dear Heavenly Father, Grow me so that your fruit will ripen in me. May I emanate love, joy, peace, long-suffering, kindness, goodness, humility, gentleness, patience and self-control. Amen.

Journal

____

____

____

____

____

Day 225

Forgive as the Lord forgave you. And over all these virtues, put on love, which binds them all together in perfect unity. Colossians 2:13b,14

The adhesive agent for those wonderful before mentioned virtues is love. Love encompasses forgiveness. Forgiveness and love are choices we either make or reject. Our Lord's prayer mentions forgiveness - Matthew 6:12, 'Forgive us our debts as we also have forgiven our debtors.' This is a marked claim - how do you forgive others?

Prayer: Dear Heavenly Father, I pray again - Search O God and know my thoughts and ways, reveal to me any sin that may be lurking in the background of my life, so I may confess it, deal with it and receive your forgiveness. Amen.

Journal

____

____

____

____

____

Day 226

Let the peace of Christ rule in your hearts, since as members of one body you were called to peace. And be thankful. Colossians 3:15

Peace is what we as a human race most desire globally and individually. If we were at peace within ourselves, there would be less unrest in our community and country. Peace replaces bitterness and verbal combativeness. How do you obtain inner peace? Do you rest in the arms of Jesus and tell him all that is on your heart and in your life? Do you listen to peaceful praise and worship music? Have you surrended your hurts to Jesus?

Prayer: Dear Heavenly Father, You are my peace, you have broken down every bondage chain. Thank you for your resurrection power in my life. I trust in you, my Lord, for sustaining peace and rest in you. Amen.

Journal

____

____

____

____

____

Day 227

Let the message of Christ dwell among you richly as you teach and admonish one another with all wisdom, through psalms, hymns and songs from the spirit, singing to God with gratitude in your hearts. Colossians 3:16

Christian music and songs is a powerful medium in which we can focus on Christ Jesus. We worship and praise him through these spiritual songs, the melodies and words linger with us throughout the days and nights. Do you listen to positive music as you drive in your car, in your home, as you exercise or any other time? Praise God for these pleasant ways we can focus our thoughts and emotions on our wonderful Savior, Christ Jesus.

Prayer: Dear Heavenly Father, Singing Hallelujah, praise and worship to my Lord. I lift my voice in song up to you, I lift my hands to reach out to you. I lift my heart to tell you I love you. Singing Hallelujah, praise and worship to my Lord. Amen.

Journal

____

____

____

____

____

Day 228

And whatever you do, whether in word or deed, do it all in the name of the Lord Jesus, giving thanks to God the Father through him. Colossians 3:17

Our hope is built on nothing less than Jesus' blood and righteousness - this stanza is from an old hymn. It is Jesus who is our standard, it is he who has redeemed us. He is the focus in our lives, the one whom we look to for all our needs. Let us honor him in our attitude, speech and actions. He is worthy, he is King, he is Lord of our lives. Spend time in praise and worship towards your wonderfully kind and loving Lord.

Today sing the old hymn, Our hope is built on nothing less, than Jesus' blood and righteousness.

Journal

____

____

____

____

Day 229

Wives, submit yourselves to your husbands, as is fitting in the Lord. Husbands, love your wives and do not be harsh with them. Children, obey your parents in everything, for this pleased the Lord. Fathers, do not embitter your children, or they will become discouraged. Colossians 3:18-21

Special instructions for a family, with emphasis placed on the men - towards their wives and towards their children. I wonder what this world would look like if all or most families were functioning as described in the Biblical passages. There would be less divorces, less single parenthood, less sexual confusion, less murders. PRAY FOR RESTORATION OF FAMILIES.

Prayer: Dear Heavenly Father, What a mess we have made of families in our present society. What a mess sin had created so there are dads, moms and kids who are fighting one another, or there are no dads in the family, or both parents are absent either physically or emotionally. I know you know. It is not a surprise to you. I pray for restoration of people to come to know you, and I pray for the restoration of healthy families. Amen.

Journal

____

____

____

____

____

Day 230

Slaves, obey your earthly masters in everything; and do it, not only when their eye is on you and to curry their favor, but with sincerity of heart and reverence for the Lord. Whatever you do, work at it with all your heart, as working for the Lord, not for human masters, since you know that you will receive an inheritance from the Lord as a reward. It is the Lord Christ you are serving. Colossians 3:22-24

We can think of this situation in our days as a boss/employee/instructor relationship, in attitude but not ownership. We are instructed to do our tasks as if we are doing them with and for our Lord.

Prayer: Dear Heavenly Father, Help me to shine for you in my place of learning or work each day. May I be pleasant, honest and kind to my teachers and/or boss. Amen.

Journal

____

____

____

____

____

Day 231

Anyone who does wrong will be repaid for their wrongs, and there is no favoritism. Masters, provide your slaves with what is right and fair, because you know that you also have a Master in heaven. Colossians 3:25, 4:1

Paul tells both slaves and masters to show Christian principles in their relationships with their slaves. The call is for us as well - to show Christian principles in our relationships, particularly in subservient relationships. An old children's Bible song states - 'He sees all I do, he hears all I say, My God is listening all the time.' Let us be transparent before God in our relationships toward him and others, so He will shine through us.

Prayer: Dear Heavenly Father, Keep me true to you in my relationships, that I may be your mouth, eyes, ears, hands and feet as I work alongside others. Amen.

Journal

____

____

____

____

____

Day 232

Devote yourselves to prayer, being watchful and thankful. And pray for us, too, that God may open a door for our message, so that we may proclaim the mystery of Christ, for which I am in chains. Pray that I may proclaim it clearly, as I should. Colossians 4:2-4

Paul is asking for prayer, and in essence he sets a great example for our prayers for each other. To be watchful, thankful and a clear message of the gospel to emulate from our lips and our lives.

Prayer: Dear Heavenly Father, I offer myself as a willing vessel to spread the gospel to my friends and acquaintances who do not know you. Amen.

Journal

____

____

____

____

____

Day 233

Be wise in the way you act toward outsiders; make the most of every opportunity. Let your conversation be always full of grace, seasoned with salt, so that you may know how to answer everyone. Colossians 4:5,6

The Bible is full of verses encouraging us to 'guard our tongue.' Out of the mouth comes what is brewing in the heart. Ask the Lord to check your heart and mind, surrender them to him. Ask for the Fruit of the Spirit (Galatians 5:22,23) to emulate from you in your thoughts, speech and actions.

Prayer: Dear Heavenly Father, guard my mind, my heart and my mouth. May my speech be full of grace, seasoned with salt, so that you will be glorified and others edified. Amen.

Journal

Day 234

Tychicus will tell you all the news about me. He is a dear brother, a faithful minister and fellow servant in the Lord. I am sending him to you for the express purpose that you may know about our circumstances and that he may encourage your hearts. He is coming with Onesimus, our faithful and dear brother, who is one of you. They will tell you everything that is happening here. Colossians 4:7-9

Many names mentioned in this passage are also mentioned in Philemon, which may suggest both letters could have been written at the same time. We also see Paul's love and care for his brothers in the Lord, and the church at Colossae.

Prayer: Dear Heavenly Father, thank you for the friends you have put in my life. I particularly thank you for (name the person or people) and the blessing they have been to me. Thank you for their faithful service to them. Bless them richly. Amen.

Journal

____

____

____

____

____

Day 235

My fellow prisoner Aristarchus sends you his greetings, as does Mark, the cousin of Barnabas. (You have received instructions about him; if he comes to you welcome him). Jesus, who is called Justus, also sends greeting. These are the only Jews among my co-workers for the kingdom of God, and they have proved a comfort to me.

We see a genuine brotherhood in Paul's description of his friends. It tends to make one do a little introspection about what we say about our friends and how we treat them.

Prayer: Dear Heavenly Father, I continue to pray for more friends today. I pray for (name the friends) and thank you for their influence in my life, and the example they are to me. Bless them richly. Amen.

Journal

____

____

____

____

____

Day 236

Epaphras, who is one of you and a servant of Christ Jesus, sends greetings. He is always wrestling in prayer for you, that you may stand firm in all the will of God, mature and fully assured. I vouch for him that he is working hard for you and for those at Laodicea and Hierapolis. Colossians 4:12,13

Paul's salutations usually end with greetings from friends and some insight as to their relationship to either Paul, or, the church, or both. Today and tomorrow continue to consider and pray for your friends, identifying who they are, what they mean to you. Make a purposeful effort to love on, them as you pray for them.

Prayer: Dear Heavenly Father, I continue to pray for more friends today. I pray for (*name the friends*) and thank you for their influence in my life, and the example they are to me. Bless them richly. Amen.

Journal

____

____

____

____

____

Day 237

Our dear friend Luke, the doctor, and Demas send greetings. Give my greetings to the brothers and sisters at Laodicea, and to Nympha and the church in her house. Colossians 4:14,15

Again, spend time making a list of your friends, your blessings together and special prayers for each one. Pray your prayers for them, forgiving as necessary. Love on the through the power given to you through the Holy Spirit. Give yourself time, in thankfulness, before the Lord, nestling into him, enjoying his love and care toward you.

Prayer: Dear Heavenly Father, I continue to pray for more friends today. I pray for (*name the friends*) and thank you for their influence in my life, and the example they are to me. Bless them richly. Amen.

Journal

Day 238

After this letter has been read to you, see that it is also read in the church of the Laodiceans and that you in turn read the letter from Laodicea. Tell Archippus: See to it that you complete the ministry you have received in the Lord. I, Paul, write this greeting in my own hand. Remember my chains. Grace be with you. Colossians 4:16-18

Paul's letters were circulated around the churches in Asia Minor (present day Turkey). Much of the content was for the Christian population as a whole, with a few personal attachments. They still are anointed today for us to read, assimilate and follow.

Prayer: Dear Heavenly Father, Thank you for your word, inspired by men and women who love you, those many years ago, and which is still pertinent today. Thank you that your word is fresh and new to us each morning, and carried us through our days, until we meet you. Amen.

Journal

Day 239

Paul, Silas and Timothy, To the church of the Thessalonians in God the Father and the Lord Jesus Christ: Grace and peace to you. We always thank God for all of you and continually mention you in our prayers. We remember before our God and Father your work produced by faith, your labor prompted by love, and your endurance inspired by hope in our Lord Jesus Christ. 1 Thessalonians 1:1-3

These scriptures are beautiful examples of prayers for our friends, families and fellow believers. The triad of faith, love and hope are expanded and used in the prayer. Take them and pray for your family, friends and fellow Christians, embellishing each with prayer.

Prayer: Dear Heavenly Father, I pray for my family, friends and acquaintances (name them), and ask that you remember their work produced by faith, their labor prompted by love and their endurance inspired by hope in our Lord Jesus. Bless each of them today. Amen.

Journal

____

____

____

____

____

Day 240

For we know, brothers and sisters loved by God, that he has chosen you, because our gospel came to you not simply with words but also with power, with the Holy Spirit and deep conviction. You know how we lived among you for your sake. You became imitators of us and of the Lord, for you welcomed the message in the midst of severe suffering with the joy given by the Holy Spirit. 1 Thessalonians 1:4-6

These people received the truth of the Gospel and freedom from the bondage of sin through Christ Jesus as we do. Paul, Silas and Timothy lived among them for a time and mentoring and discipling them for a life of trusting Christ Jesus.

Prayer: Dear Heavenly Father, no matter what is happening or where I am, you are there with me by your Holy Spirit. Thank you for the promise that you will never leave, nor forsake me. I trust in you. Amen.

Journal

____

____

____

____

____

Day 241

And so, you became a model to all the believers in Macedonia and Achaia. The Lord's message rang out from you not only in Macedonia and Achaia - your faith in God has become known everywhere. Therefore, we do not need to say anything about it, for they themselves report what kind of reception you gave us. They tell how you turned to God from idols to serve the living and true God, and to wait for his Son from heaven, whom he raised from the dead - Jesus, who rescues us from the coming wrath. I Thessalonians 1:7-10

Amen and Amen. Let our light shine in this dark world as these christians did.

Prayer: Dear Heavenly Father, Let my light shine for you in this dark world. May I be that beacon of hope drawing others to you. Let my eyes, ears, mouth, hands and feet be representatives for you today. Amen.

Journal

Day 242

You know, brothers and sisters, that our visit to you was not without results. We had previously suffered and been treated outrageously in Philippi, as you know, but with the help of our God we dared to tell you his gospel in the face of strong opposition. I Thessalonians 2:1,2

See Acts 16:19-40 for context. Isn't it interesting to see that Paul and his fellow workers continued spreading the good news of Jesus Christ despite opposition - some of the opposition being life threatening. It causes us to ask the question about our zeal for spreading the Gospel in our society which is antagonistic to the ways of God and his truth.

Prayer: Dear Heavenly Father, Give me strength, courage and opportunity to spread your good news to needy people you put in my life. May I be bold and speak the truth for you. Amen.

Journal

____

____

____

____

____

Day 243

For the appeal we make does not spring from error or impure motives, nor are we trying to trick you. On the contrary, we speak as those approved by God to be entrusted with the Gospel. We are not trying to please people but God, who tests our hearts. You know we never used flattery, nor did we put on a mask to cover up greed - God is our witness. We were not looking for praise from people, not from you nor anyone else...... 1 Thessalonians 2:3-6a

Paul explains that he and his fellow workers were and are honest, God-fearing representatives having been approved by God and entrusted with the life-giving message of the Gospel. There was, nor is, no ulterior motive.

Prayer: Dear Heavenly Father, Keep me true to you in this race of life. Keep me honest, gracious, kind and good as I represent you to this world who needs you but opposes you. Amen.

Journal

Day 244

…even though as apostles of Christ we could have asserted our authority. Instead, we were like young children among you. Just as a nursing mother cares for her children, so we cared for you. Because we loved you so much, we were delighted to share with you not only the gospel of God but our lives as well. Surely you remember, brothers and sisters, our toil and hardship; we worked night and day in order not to be a burden to anyone while we preached the gospel of God to you. 1 Thessalonians 2:6b-9

Paul and his friends (noted in the use of 'we'), supported themselves so as not to be a burden on others, i.e., they worked for their upkeep. They did this joyfully so that they would be able to spread the good news of the Gospel to people and church at Thessalonica. What extent do you go to care for those in your sphere of the world?

Prayer: Dear Heavenly Father, Give me opportunity and strength to care for those around me. I pray for *(name the person)*, please help me see their need and to extend my hand to them for your sake. Amen.

Journal

Day 245

You are witnesses, and so is God, of how holy, righteous and blameless we were among you who believed. For you know that we dealt with each of you as a father deals with his own children, encouraging, comforting and urging you to live lives worthy of God, who calls you into his kingdom and glory. 1 Thessalonians 2:10-12

Here is a picture of a caring relationship with friends among friends. Let it be an example to us as we care for those around us.

Prayer: Dear Heavenly Father, open my heart and mind to those around me so I can reach out to them for you, in your love. Amen.

Journal

____
____
____
____
____

Day 246

And we also thank God continually because, when you received the word of God, which you heard from us, you accepted it not as a human word, but as it actually is, the word of God, which is indeed at work in you who believe. For you, brothers and sisters, became imitators of God's churches in Judea, which are in Christ Jesus: You suffered from your own people the same things those churches suffered from the Jews who killed the Lord Jesus and the prophets, and also drove us out. 1 Thessalonians 2:13-15a

Persecution of the church of Christ Jesus still persists today. Pray for the persecuted church in our day. Align yourself with organizations that pray for and support those who are persecuted, in our country and in countries of this world.

Prayer: Dear Heavenly Father, I pray for persecuted christians in the world today. *(Name people you are aware of who are being persecuted, as well as countries who are openly opposed to the word of God)*. Give them hope, strength, power, grace, and love so they can withstand the 'blows', and at the same time witness for you. May they have access to food, water, and a safe place to rest. Amen.

Journal

____

____

____

____

____

Day 247

They displease God and are hostile to everyone in their effort to keep us from speaking to the Gentiles so they may be saved. In this way they always heap up their sins to the limit. The wrath of God has come upon them at last. 1 Thessalonians 2:15b,16

We also live in a world where christians are made fun of, ridiculed, mocked and killed. Our societies are anti God and pro humanism. It's all about 'me' and my wants! It is very easy for christians to fall into the trap of humanism. Ask God to search your heart, and whatever comes up, deal with it, thank and praise God for his faithfulness and healing.

Prayer: Dear Heavenly Father, Search my heart and show me the areas where I need to confess to you. Keep me true to you. I love you. Amen.

Journal

____

____

____

____

____

Day 248

But, brothers and sisters, when we were orphaned by being separated from you for a short time (in person, not in thought), out of our intense longing we made every effort to see you. For we wanted to come to you - certainly I, Paul, did, again and again - but satan blocked our way. For what is our hope, our joy, or the crown in which we will glory in the presence of our Lord Jesus when he comes? Is it not you? Indeed, you are our glory and joy. 1 Thessalonians 2:17,18

True christian love and fellowship includes positive and honest relationships, and that of working and being together, enjoying our Lord together. As well as doing those things he has asked us to do, such as serving, learning, praying, evangelism and just doing life together.

Prayer: Dear Heavenly Father, we are all part of your body, working together for the body to function as it should. I want to do my part. Help me keep good attitudes and joy before me, and pride, jealousy and envy behind me. Amen.

Journal

____
____
____
____
____

Day 249

So, when we could stand it no longer, we thought it best to be left by ourselves in Athens. We sent Timothy, who is our brother and co-worker in God's service in spreading the gospel of Christ, to strengthen and encourage you in your faith, so that no one would be unsettled by these trials. For you know quite well that we are destined for them. 1 Thessalonians 3:1-3

Paul alludes to the persecutions and trials which the church in Thessalonica were experiencing. History tells us that since christianity is opposite to earthly philosophies of deception, all christians in all ages have experienced opposition. Today, pray for strength for yourself and other christians to stand up for what is right.

Prayer: Dear Heavenly Father, I ask you give christians strength to stand up for what is right. Begin with me in my heart, Lord. I choose to stand up for you and be that light upon the hill, shining for you. Amen.

Journal

____

____

____

____

____

Day 250

In fact, when we were with you, we kept telling you that we would be persecuted. And it turned out that way, as you well know. For this reason, when I could stand it no longer, I sent to find out about your faith. I was afraid that in some way the tempter had tempted you and that our labors might have been in vain. 1 Thessalonians 3:4,5

Paul reaches out to his friends in love and concern. We are reminded in the verse,

1 John 4:4b 'The one who is in you, is greater that the one who is in the world.' Our Lord Jesus Christ is on our side, and he has already won the battle for us - through his death and resurrection. Praise his name.

Prayer: Dear Heavenly Father, You are the Lord of Lord, King of Kings, the Alpha and Omega, the High King of Heaven, my Savior, my Redeemer, my joy and my victor. I am blessed.

Journal

____

____

____

____

____

Day 251

But Timothy has just now come to us from you and has brought good news about your faith and love. He has told us that you always have pleasant memories of us and that you long to see us, just as we long to see you. Therefore, brothers and sisters, in all our distress and persecution we were encouraged about you because of your faith.   1 Thessalonians 3:6,7

The persecution or sufferings were worth the pain to see the resulting love and faith of those in the church at Thessalonica. Often the Lord puts us through difficult situations to birth newness. In this case it was growth in the individuals and the church. What is it in your case? Journal your thoughts.

Prayer: Dear Heavenly Father, thank you for birthing in me (*name your situations which produced the fruit of the Spirit*). I rely on you to always be with me, as you have promised. Amen.

Journal

____

____

____

____

____

Day 252

For now, we really live, since you are standing firm in the Lord. How can we thank God enough for you in return for all the joy we have in the presence of our God because of you? Night and Day we pray most earnestly that we may see you again and supply what is lacking in your faith. 1 Thessalonians 3:8-10

Here we see a caring friend, teacher, father, delighted to know the faithful converts are standing firm, and growing in their love and knowledge of Christ Jesus.

Prayer: Dear Heavenly Father, teach me to care for others the way I should. Help me to see others through your eyes and not my self-serving person. Amen.

Journal

____
____
____
____
____

Day 253

Now may our God and Father himself and our Lord Jesus clear the way for us to come to you. May the Lord make your love increase and overflow for each other and for everyone else, just as ours does for you. May he strengthen your hearts so that you will be blameless and holy in the presence of our God and Father when our Lord Jesus comes with all his holy ones. 1 Thessalonians 3:11-13

To reiterate Paul 's words - may 'our' love increase and overflow for each other and for everyone else! Ponder the statement and Journal its meaning to you.

Pray over your Journal entries and for the dear ones in your life. Ask the Lord to put love in your heart for those 'outside' the faith.

Journal

____

____

____

____

Day 254

As for other matters, brothers and sisters, we instructed you how to live in order to please God, as in fact you are living. Now we ask you and urge you in the Lord Jesus to do this more and more. For you know what instructions we gave you by the authority of the Lord Jesus. I Thessalonians 4:1,2

The church at Thessolinica is encouraged regarding their lives set apart for Jesus, and they are urged to continue to follow the footsteps of their savior. We also are encouraged and urged to follow Christ's example and footsteps as spoken about in the Word of God.

Prayer: Dear Heavenly Father, Lord, I lift my hands toward heaven reaching out to you, and I reach out my hands out to those around me to serve you and share your love with them. Amen.

Journal

Day 255

It is God's will that you should be sanctified: that you should avoid sexual immorality; that each of you should learn to control your own body in a way that is holy and honorable, not in passionate lust like the pagans, who do not know God; and that in this matter no one should wrong or take advantage of a brother or sister. The Lord will punish all those who commit such sins, as we told you and warned you before. 1 Thessalonians 4:3-6

It is a fact that sexual sin harms others besides those who engage in it. For example, in adultery, the spouse is always wronged; in premarital sex, or fornication, it wrongs the future partner by taking from him or her of the virginity that ought to be brought into marriage. Oh dear, our world definitely fails on this one!

Prayer: Dear Heavenly Father, I want to remain true to you and your word. *(offer confession and ask for forgiveness in this matter if you need to).* Keep my eyes on you and my ears hearing your voice. Help me not to stray into the deceptive teachings of this world. Amen.

Journal

Day 256

Now about your love for one another we do not need to write to you, for you yourselves have been taught by God to love each other. And in fact, you do love all God's family throughout Macedonia. Yet we urge you, brothers and sisters, to do so more and more,... 1 Thessalonians 4:9,10

Brotherly love means love for other christians. We are one body working together. We are a family - a family is in relationship. Christian and family love means to care for each other, pray for each other, and serve together. See 1 John 4:12, others will see God through the love of his disciples.

Prayer: Dear Heavenly Father, may my love show through the way I care for others. Please shine through me. Give me a heart of love for those around me. Amen.

Journal

____

____

____

____

____

Day 257

...and to make it your ambition to lead a quiet life: You should mind your own business and work with your hands, just as we told you, so that your daily life may win the respect of outsiders and so that you will not be dependent on anybody. 1 Thessalonians 4:11,12

The advise Paul is sharing is pertinent for our current situations. Be found 'doing' and not 'idling'. You are more productive and your mind is occupied with your work processes when you are found 'doing'. Ask the Lord to keep your mind focused on Him.

Prayer: Dear Heavenly Father, Keep my mind focused on you and the job you have given me to do. I do not want to be idle or a busybody. Find me doing your work. Amen.

Journal

____

____

____

____

Day 258

Brothers and sisters, we do not want you to be uninformed about those who sleep in death, so that you do not grieve like the rest of mankind, who have no hope. For we believe that Jesus died and rose again, and so we believe that God will bring with Jesus those who have fallen asleep in him. 1 Thessalonians 4:13,14

Paul begins his eschatological dialogue with the Thessalonians, who were living the misunderstanding that Christ's return is imminent - very soon. He assures them that those who have died before the second coming of Jesus Christ, will be with Christ now, and we will see them again. He uses words such as 'asleep' or 'sleep' for death. Are you prepared to pass from this realm, into the realm of God's glory, through death? Are you ready for your day?

Prayer: Dear Heavenly Father, yes, Lord, I am ready for you to come again. However, I do not want to be found idle. Keep me in your service working for your Kingdom while I am on this earth. Amen.

Journal

____

____

____

____

____

Day 259

According to the Lord's word, we tell you that we who are still alive, who are left until the coming of the Lord, will certainly not precede those who have fallen asleep. For the Lord himself will come down from heaven, with a loud command, with the voice of the archangel and with the trumpet call of God, and the dead in Christ will rise first.   1 Thessalonians 4:15,16

It is thought that the mention of 'the Lord's word', were either an oral tradition passed down to believers, or a direct revelation to Paul. Whatever it means, does not deter from the fact that Jesus is coming back to this earth to receive all those who follow him, and take them back to heaven to live there with him for eternity. Will you be there?

Prayer: Dear Heavenly Father, Yes, I will be there with you. Thank you for loving me enough to send Jesus to this earth as my redeemer and savior and saving me from the curse of sin. Amen.

Journal

____

____

____

____

____

Day 260

After that, we who are still alive and are left will be caught up together with them in the clouds to meet the Lord in the air. And so we will be with the Lord forever. Therefore, encourage one another with these words. 1 Thessalonians 4:17,18

The event of the second coming appears to be open and obvious to all who are on earth, with the sound of the voice of the archangel and trumpet sound - rather than a secretive occasion, as some have chosen to believe. It will be a joyous and momentous occasion, the hope of all christians - to be taken to heaven and spend eternity with our Lord and Savior.

Prayer: Dear Heavenly Father, I am humbly grateful to be one who will be with you for eternity. Thank you for rescuing me. Amen.

Journal

____

____

____

____

____

Day 261

Now, brothers and sisters, about times and dates we do not need to write to you, for you know very well that the day of the Lord will come like a thief in the night. While people are saying, 'Peace and safety,' destruction will come on them suddenly, as labor pains on a pregnant woman, and they will not escape. 1 Thessalonians 5:1-3

See 1 Corinthians 5:5 for another mention about the day of the Lord'. This expression goes back to Amos 5:18, when God will come to intervene with judgement and/or blessing. This day is either a day of judgment or a day of redemption, depending on who you are following - Jesus or yourself!

Prayer: Dear Heavenly Father, I pray for the spread of your Gospel in this sad world. May your Holy Spirit move throughout this world convicting people of their sin. May I be of use to you to be your voice, eyes, ears, hands and feet to bring the good news to those around me. Amen.

Journal

____

____

____

____

____

Day 262

But you, brothers and sisters, are not in darkness so that this day should surprise you like a thief. You are all children of the light and children of the day. We do not belong to the night or to the darkness. So then, let us not be like others, who are asleep, but let us be awake and sober. For those who sleep, sleep at night, and those who get drunk, get drunk at night. 1 Thessalonians 5:4-7

Unbelievers are spiritually unaware - or asleep. Often, people choose to be drunk or unaware in order not to face truth and change. It is as if they are hiding from truth and change. Some people are in denial about their habits or behavior, and have not been aware of the Holy Spirit's prodding, or, are pushing the Holy Spirit away.

Prayer: Dear Heavenly Father, today I pray for those in my family of sphere of friends, *(name them)*, who are struggling with these things. Give them strength to face the issues, and faith to trust you for their redemption. Amen.

Journal

Day 263

But since we belong to the day, let us be sober, putting on faith and love as a breastplate, and the hope of salvation as a helmet. For God did not appoint us to suffer wrath but to receive salvation through our Lord Jesus Christ. 1 Thessalonians 5:8,9

When we live in the 'day', all is exposed. Our Lord wants us to live honest lives with integrity. We are not phonies, but true to our commitment to Christ for all to see - to live a life of faith, hope and love in our Lord Jesus Christ.

Prayer: Dear Heavenly Father, Keep me true to you in this race of life. I want to grow to be more like you, in all that I do say and think. Amen.

Journal

___

Day 264

He died for us so that, whether we are awake or asleep, we may live together with him. Therefore encourage one another and build each other up, just as in fact you are doing. 1 Thessalonians 5:10-11

As a christian, we have the hope of eternal life, i.e., life on earth and in heaven with our Lord. The relationship we have with Jesus Christ will never end. He wants us to start living as a family, 'the body of Christ', on earth before we enter our heavenly dwelling and to encourage and build each other up in 'him'. How do we do that? By praying and caring for each other through healthy relationships, trust, service together, worshipping together, hospitality, etc. Today, pray for the church here on earth.

Prayer: Dear Heavenly Father, I pray for your family, the church, here on earth today, and my church. I pray that the Leaders will hear you speak to them and will willingly follow your direction as you have laid out to them. Give them a double portion of the fruits of the Spirit, to love on those you send their way. Amen.

Journal

____

____

____

____

____

Day 265

Now we ask you, brothers and sisters, to acknowledge those who work hard among you, who care for you in the Lord and who admonish you. Hold them in the highest regard in love because of their work. Live in peace with each other. And we urge you, brothers and sisters, warn those who are idle and disruptive, encourage the disheartened, help the weak, be patient with everyone. 1 Thessalonians 5:12-14

Wise words from Paul to his beloved church at Thessalonica, and to us! Respect those who are in authority, love them, and each other. Live lives of helpful busyness and patience.

Prayer: Dear Heavenly Father, Thank you for your gift of peace. Peace in my heart throughout the day and at night, especially when I wake during the night. Amen.

Journal

____
____
____
____
____

Day 266

Make sure that nobody pays back wrong for wrong, but always strive to do what is good for each other and for everyone else. Rejoice always, pray continually, give thanks in all circumstances; for this is God's will for you in Christ Jesus. 1 Thessalonians 5:15-18

Retaliation is out of the question for a christian - instead we are to love on and be kind to the offender. Pray for them and for each other, giving thanks in all things - even the bad. How is your prayer life? Do you have a regular appointment with the Lord? Do you have a Journal for prayer requests and answers? Remember there are three answers to prayer - no, with and yes. They are all answers.

Prayer: Dear Heavenly Father, thank you for my family and friends, I appreciate each of them. I pray for *(name your family and friends)* and ask you help them each with their issues *(name the issues)*. Amen.

Journal

____

____

____

____

____

Day 267

Do not quench the Spirit. Do not treat prophecies with contempt but test them all; hold on to what is good, reject every kind of evil. 1 Thessalonians 5:19-22

These words written to the church at Thessalonica are also directed to christians past and present. Allow the Holy Spirit to influence your attitudes, activities and relationships. Read the Holy Bible and assimilate the truths spoken in the inspired texts. Keep your heart and mind clean and clear for God to speak to you.

Prayer: Dear Heavenly Father, I want to live my life for you in faith and truth. Please show me if there is anything in me that would take that away from our relationship. Keep my mind clean and clear so I can hear your voice. Amen.

Journal

____

____

____

____

____

Day 268

May God himself, the God of peace, sanctify you through and through. May your whole spirit, soul and body be kept blameless at the coming of our Lord Jesus Christ. <u>The one who calls you is faithful, and he will do it.</u> Brothers and sisters, pray for us. Greet all God's people with a holy kiss. I charge you before the Lord to have this letter read to all the brothers and sisters. The grace of our Lord Jesus Christ be with you. 1 Thessalonians 5:23-28

We are to have faith, belief and confidence that the Lord will 'complete' those promises which have been made. In your Journal, list promises you have claimed and the outworking of them you have seen. Thank and praise God.

Today, sing the old hymn, Count your blessings, name them one by one.

Journal

____

____

____

____

____

Day 269

To the church of the Thessalonians in God our Father and the Lord Jesus Christ: Grace and peace to you from God the Father and the Lord Jesus Christ. 2 Thessalonians 1:1,2

The blessing extends to you, in your life and situation. Our Lord reaches out to you in grace (an unmerited gift) and peace. Recognize the Lord in your situation(s), and reach out to touch him. Rest in his love toward you.

Prayer: Dear Heavenly Father, thank you for your love to me. Thank you that you know my name and my situation. There is nothing that you do not know about me, and I am at rest and peace about you knowing my being. I trust you and nestle into you. I love you. Amen.

Journal

____

____

____

____

____

Day 270

We ought always to thank God for you, brothers and sisters, and rightly so, because your faith is growing more and more, and the love all of you have for one another is increasing. Therefore, among God's churches we boast about your perseverance and faith in all the persecutions and trials you are enduring. 2 Thessalonians 1:3,4

Persecutions and trials either strengthen our faith or leave us dismayed. It is our choice as to which will be the outcome. Choose faith in Jesus Christ - he did tell us 'in this life you will have trouble', John 16:33, but we are to resist the devil and run into Jesus our savior, for peace, hope, direction and security.

Prayer: Dear Heavenly Father, thank you for always being 'there' for me. I can run to the safety of your arms and find peace. Amen.

Journal

____

____

____

____

____

Day 271

All this is evidence that God's judgment is right, and as a result you will be counted worthy of the kingdom of God, for which you are suffering. God is just: He will pay back trouble to those who trouble you and give relief to you who are troubled, and to us as well. 2 Thessalonians 1:5-7a

What is the 'evidence' Paul is talking about? It is in the way the Thessalonians endured trials. God did not leave them to their own resources. He provided strength to endure, and this in turn produced spiritual and moral character, as he does for us. It also proved that God was on their side and gave warning to their persecutors, again, as he does for us. This message is for you as well as for the readers of Paul's letter.

Prayer: Dear Heavenly Father, you know all that is happening in this world, and in my life. I know you are with me and I thank you for the relief you provide. Amen.

Journal

____

____

____

____

____

Day 272

This will happen when the Lord Jesus is revealed from heaven in blazing fire with his powerful angels. He will punish those who do not know God and do not obey the gospel of our Lord Jesus. 2 Thessalonians 1:7b-8

The Bible is clear that there is going to be a 'reckoning' in the future, when Jesus returns to earth with his myriad of powerful angels to call his people to him - dead and alive; to live with him forever. As christians, he has commanded us to tell the world of the wonderful plan of salvation, which is good news to a degenerate world - it is available to everyone.

Prayer: Dear Heavenly Father, your plan of salvation was and is perfect. Jesus showed us how to live for you in a human form. Thank you for his example to us. Thank you for salvation. Amen.

Journal

____

____

____

____

____

Day 273

They will be punished with everlasting destruction and shut out from the presence of the Lord and from the glory of his might on the day he comes to be glorified in his holy people and to be marveled at among all those who have believed. This includes you, because you believed our testimony to you.
2 Thessalonians 1:9,10

The penalty of sin is eternal separation from God. The reward of salvation is the eternal presence with God. As christians, our job is to spread the gospel, so our fellow mankind will have eternal presence with God. See Matthew 19:28,29.

Prayer: Dear Heavenly Father, I pray for and reach out in love to those around you who do not know you. Lead me to the specific ones today. Amen.

Journal

____
____
____
____
____

Day 274

With this in mind, we constantly pray for you, that our God may make you worthy of his calling, and that by his power he may bring to fruition your every desire for goodness and your every deed prompted by faith. We pray this so that the name of our Lord Jesus may be glorified in you, and you in him, according to the grace of our God and the Lord Jesus Christ. 2 Thessalonians 1:11,12

Paul and his friends set a wonderful example of praying for each other.

Prayer: Dear Heavenly Father, I continue praying for my friends and acquaintances. Help me to reach out to them in love. Let me find them open and ready to receive the good news. Amen.

Journal

____
____
____
____
____

Day 275

Concerning the coming of our Lord Jesus Christ and our being gathered to him, we ask you, brothers and sisters, not to become easily unsettled or alarmed by the teaching allegedly from us - whether by a prophecy or by word of mouth or by letter - asserting that the day of the Lord has already come. 2 Thessalonians 2:1,2

It seems as though, in the days Paul is talking about, there was some sort of conspiracy theory, as we have experienced today. This theory was about the Lord having already come - which Paul is refuting. As christians, we need to align what we hear to what the Word of God states and ask our pertinent questions on that basis.

Prayer: Dear Heavenly Father, Keep me in the truth of your word. Keep your word shining as a lamp to my feet, showing me my steps, and a light to my path showing me the big picture. Amen.

Journal

———————————————————————————————————

———————————————————————————————————

———————————————————————————————————

———————————————————————————————————

———————————————————————————————————

Day 276

Don't let anyone deceive you in any way, for that day will not come until the rebellion occurs and the man of lawlessness is revealed, the man doomed to destruction. He will oppose and will exalt himself over everything that is called God, or is worshiped, so that he sets himself up in God's temple, proclaiming himself to be God. 2 Thessalonians 2:3,4

Ugh! Rebellion is likened to the falling away from faith in Jesus Christ. The 'man of lawlessness' is the antichrist spoken about in Revelation 13:1-10. He is a man who is not only a political and military figure, but he sets himself up as a god as well. All this has to happen before the great day in which Jesus returns.

Prayer: Dear Heavenly Father, keep me watchful and sober minded so that I will not fall into the traps of the evil one. Keep mindful of you and keep me from deception. Amen.

Journal

____

____

____

____

____

Day 277

Don't you remember that when I was with you I used to tell you these things? And now you know what is holding him back, so that he may be revealed at the proper time. For the secret power of lawlessness is already at work; but the one who now holds it back will continue to do so till he is taken out of the way. 2 Thessalonians 2:5-7

Evil is already in this world, and it is being held back until it is time for 'all to be revealed' at the Lord's second coming. One could say our present times evidence lawlessness, with tyrannical powers, 'rights' movements, lack of morals and absolutes and evil. Pray for our county, our country, and other countries.

Prayer: Dear Heavenly Father, I pray for *(name your country)* that you will shake us up to see where we stand with you. Expose evil for what it is. Expose corruption in high places. Search our hearts so we will make things right with you. Bring a revival to faith in you and begin the revival in me. Amen.

Journal

____

____

____

____

____

Day 278

And then the lawless one will be revealed, whom the Lord Jesus will overthrow with the breath of his mouth and destroy by the splendor of his coming. The coming of the lawless one will be in accordance with how satan works. He will use all sorts of displays of power through signs and wonders that serve the lie, and all the ways that wickedness deceives those who are perishing. 2 Thessalonians 2:8-10a

Not a pretty picture. Note the lawless one will be easily destroyed - by the power of the breath of Christ. (Remembering, he spoke creation into place, see Genesis 1). Our God can do anything. He works outside of our physical constraints - He is God.

Prayer: Dear Heavenly Father, I pray for those in my life who are sucked into the deception of this world. Pray for salvation for *(name your family, friends, acquaintances)*.

I want to be your eyes, ears, mouth, hands and feet toward them today to encourage them about you. Amen.

Journal

____

____

____

____

Day 279

They perish because they refuse to love the truth and so be saved. For this reason God sends them a powerful delusion so that they will believe the lie and so that all will be condemned who have not believed the truth but have delighted in wickedness. 2 Thessalonians 2:10b-12

Sometimes the Lord uses sin to punish the sinful. Here, in this case, he uses delusion, or a lie, so that they will be condemned - they will believe that the antichrist is God Almighty. Oh my, what a travesty.

Prayer: Dear Heavenly Father, I pray that my loved ones, friends and acquaintances will believe the truth and not the convenience of the lie, which the antichrist expects from them. I believe that the Lord Jesus Christ is God. Amen

Journal

____

____

____

____

____

Day 280

But we ought always to thank God for you, brothers and sisters loved by the Lord, because God chose you as first fruits to be saved through the sanctifying work of the Spirit and through belief in the truth. He called you to this through our gospel, that you might share in the glory of our Lord Jesus Christ. 2 Thessalonians 2:13,14

As with the Thessalonian church, you and I have been chosen 'from the beginning' and have been called by God to share in the glory of the Lord Jesus Christ. In the meantime, we have work to do, as his glory is shining through us.

Prayer: Dear Heavenly Father, Keep me shining the truth of the gospel in this sad dark world. Amen.

Journal

____

____

____

____

____

Day 281

So then, brothers and sisters, stand firm and hold fast to the teachings we passed on to you, whether by word of mouth or by letter. May our Lord Jesus Christ himself and God our Father, who loved us and by his grace gave us eternal encouragement and good hope, encourage your hearts and strengthen you in every good deed and word. 2 Thessalonians 2:15-17

The early method of passing on information was by oral tradition, or written manuscripts. Paul refers to both here. Paul's salutation is one of encouragement and hope. May we also encourage those who are in our sphere of life each day.

Prayer: Dear Heavenly Father, thank you for loving us and giving us eternal encouragement and good hope. Thank you for strengthening me in every good deed and word. Amen.

Journal

____

____

____

____

____

Day 282

As for other matters, brothers and sisters, pray for us that the message of the Lord may spread rapidly and be honored, just as it was with you. And pray that we may be delivered from wicked and evil people, for not everyone has faith. But the Lord is faithful, and he will protect you from the evil one. 2 Thessalonians 3:1-3

Paul ends his letter with a prayer request. He writes this letter from Corinth, where things were somewhat difficult for him - see Acts 18:12-13. We all need to pray for each other, our present day is evil and christians are persecuted in many nations, with growing antagonism in the western sector as well. Pray with Paul for the rapid spread of the gospel and deliverance from evil men.

Prayer: Dear Heavenly Father, I ask that you bring revival and bring it quickly. Thank you for your Holy Spirit to comfort and lead me into all things. Keep me true to you and your word, give me strength to speak up for you. Amen.

Journal

Day 283

We have confidence in the Lord that you are doing and will continue to do the things we command. May the Lord direct your hearts into God's love and Christ's perseverance. 2 Thessalonians 4,5

Paul's prayer continues to speak to the Thessalonians, encouraging them to remain faithful to the faith and persevere, as Christ did. The prayer extends to us as well. May you be found faithful, standing up for your belief in Christ Jesus and you commitment to him. Amen.

Prayer: Dear Heavenly Father, thank you for your ever listening ear to my requests. Thank you for your love and comfort to me. Give me opportunity and strength to stand firmly for you. Amen.

Journal

____

____

____

____

Day 284

In the name of the Lord Jesus Christ, we command you, brothers and sisters, to keep away from every believer who is idle and disruptive and does not live according to the teaching you received from us. For you yourselves know how you ought to follow our example. We were not idle when we were with you, nor did we eat anyone's food without paying for it. On the contrary, we worked night and day, laboring and toiling so that we would not be a burden to any of you. 2 Thessalonians 3:6-8

Paul states in as many words, that he and his friends did not 'sponge' off the good hospitality of the Thessalonians. They worked for their living. He also has said in the next verses, that if you do not work you should not eat. He encourages everyone who is able bodied, to participate together in life, and not rely on another for basic needs to be provided by others.

Prayer: Dear Heavenly Father, Help me to be generous, honest and able to manage providing for myself. Thank you for my work or school, which I do each day. Thank you for my daily bread. Amen.

Journal

Day 285

We did this, not because we do not have the right to such help, but in order to offer ourselves as a model for you to imitate. For even when we were with you, we gave you this rule: 'The one who is unwilling to work shall not eat.'
2 Thessalonians 3:9,10

Interesting thoughts, which somewhat challenge our present welfare society. Not that we will discuss politics here. Paul is refuting the misconception some members of the church are believing - i.e., Christ's imminent return, so why work, instead wait for his return. As we exist, may we be considerate and generous to those in genuine need.

Prayer: Dear Heavenly Father, May I respond with generosity to those in genuine need. Give me a compassionate and discerning heart, to be of assistance to those in need. Amen.

Journal

____

____

____

____

____

Day 286

We hear that some among you are idle and disruptive. They are not busy; they are busybodies. Such people we command and urge in the Lord Jesus Christ to settle down and earn the food they eat. And as for you, brothers and sisters, never tire of doing what is good. 2 Thessalonians 3:11-13

It seems that these idle people were getting into others business and making a problem in the community of believers. Paul cautions against this and warns the idle and disruptive persons to get a job. Now also, we do have a society where there are many needs. A society which welcomes immigrants who are starting again from square one. A society of broken families and single parenthood - with children who are hurting. A society which is divided over morals and politics.

Prayer: Dear Heavenly Father, May I be showing your love to those who are hurting and needy around me. Help me to see them and give me the knowledge to help them with your love. Amen.

Journal

____

____

____

____

____

Day 287

Take special note of anyone who does not obey our instruction in this letter. Do not associate with them, in order that they may feel ashamed. Yet do not regard them as an enemy, but warn them as you would a fellow believer. 2 Thessalonians 3:14,15

Harsh words, however, the discipline should not be harsh but in brotherly and sisterly love. Paul knew that some folk would not accept his letter, hence inclusion of these comments. Have you ever experienced or seen people rebelling against church authority? It is not a healthy scene is it? Journal your thoughts and outcomes of the situation you have seen.

Prayer: Dear Heavenly Father, Guard me from falling away from you. Keep me grounded in your truth. Amen.

Journal

____

____

____

____

Day 288

Now may the Lord of peace himself give you peace at all times and in every way. The Lord be with all of you. I, Paul, write this greeting in my own hand, which is the distinguishing mark in all my letters. This is how I write. The grace of our Lord Jesus Christ be with you all. 2 Thessalonians 3:16-18

Paul authenticates his letter with the brief comments he makes as a salutation. His last prayer is for all of us - the grace of our Lord Jesus Christ be with you all.

Prayer: Dear Heavenly Father, thank you for your unmerited gift to me, your grace. Amen.

Journal

____
____
____
____
____

Day 289

Paul, an apostle of Christ Jesus by the command of God our Savior and of Christ Jesus our hope, to Timothy my true son in the faith: Grace, mercy and peace from God the Father and Christ Jesus our Lord. 1 Timothy 1:1,2

Would you like to receive a letter with a greeting such as Paul sent to Timothy. There is a lot of relationship and respect indicated in all those statements. Today, think about and pray for those in your life whom you love and respect, and tell them of your feelings and thoughts.

Prayer: Dear Heavenly Father, thank you for *(name those people whom you love and respect)* being in my life. I love and respect them and am grateful for you blessing me with wonderful men and women in my life. Amen.

Journal

____

____

____

____

Day 290

As I urged you when I went to Macedonia, stay there in Ephesus so that you may command certain people not to teach false doctrines any longer or to devote themselves to myths and endless genealogies. Such things promote controversial speculations rather than advancing God's work - which is by faith. The goal of this command is love, which comes from a pure heart and a good conscience and sincere faith. 1 Timothy 1:3-5

The church at Ephesus was dealing with gnosticism and asceticism. Timothy was instructed to pastor the church and refute these heresies. The goal of this command was to lead and guide the church to receive the truth of the love of Christ. We too, have to lead and guide in love - Christ's love.

Prayer: Dear Heavenly Father, your love is never ending, unfathomable, eternal, and sacrificial. Thank you for your love directed toward me. Thank you for seeing, me, seeking me, and drawing me into your family. I love you. Amen.

Journal

Day 291

Some have departed from these and have turned to meaningless talk. They want to be teachers of the law, but they do not know what they are talking about or what they so confidently affirm. 1 Timothy 1:6,7

Have you ever been in the presence of someone who has a pet theory, which is not based on God's word? It may be based on one verse or a couple of words in a verse? Be careful to keep your distance and don't be drawn in - no matter how convincing it seems. Be like the Bereans in Acts 17:11 who 'examined the scriptures every day to see if what Paul said was true.'

Prayer: Dear Heavenly Father, Keep me from persuasive arguments which are not correct. Keep me truly grounded in your word. Amen.

Journal

____

____

____

____

____

Day 292

We know that the law is good if one uses it properly. We also know that the law is made not for the righteous but for lawbreakers and rebels, the ungodly and sinful, the unholy and irreligious, for those who kill their fathers or mothers, for murderers, for the sexually immoral, for those practicing homosexuality, for slave traders and liars and perjurers - and for whatever else is contrary to the sound doctrine that conforms to the gospel concerning the glory of the blessed God, which he entrusted to me. 2 Timothy 1:8-11

This is quite a line up of evil - for whom the law has been given, not for the righteous but for those in the list. But! The hope of the gospel was entrusted to Paul to share to mankind, and also for us to share with those around us. See Matthew 28:18-20

Prayer: Dear Heavenly Father, I choose to share the good news to those around me. I ask for opportunities and strength to reach out to those who do not know you, with the wonderful news of salvation. Amen.

Journal

Day 293

I thank Christ Jesus our Lord, who has given me strength, that he considered me trustworthy, appointing me to his service. Even though I was once a blasphemer and a persecutor and violent man, I was shown mercy because I acted in ignorance and unbelief. 1 Timothy 1:12,13

Forgiveness is life giving. As Paul was forgiven his infractions against God, so are we, through the lavish, everlasting grace we are offered through Christ Jesus. The Lord's prayer states, 'forgive us our debts as we also have forgiven our debtors', Matthew 6:11.

We are forgiven the same way we forgive others. Forgiveness is healing.

Prayer: Dear Heavenly Father, thank you for your forgiveness. Help me to forgive others who have hurt me or have taken advantage of me. Amen.

Journal

____

____

____

____

____

Day 294

The grace of our Lord was poured out on me abundantly, along with the faith and love that are in Christ Jesus. Here is a trustworthy saying that deserves full acceptance: Christ Jesus came into the world to save sinners - of whom I am the worst. 1 Timothy 1:14,15

God's plan of salvation is perfect, and he has given us all the concepts and powers we need to live successfully in Him - grace, love, forgiveness, mercy, redemption and more. To add to our success, we are freely endowed with the fruit of the Spirit - love, joy, peace, patience, kindness, goodness, faithfulness, gentleness and self-control - Galatians 5:22,23a.

Prayer: Dear Heavenly Father, I praise you for your foresight and generous love toward me. Thank you for the gifts you have given me, and the fruit of the spirit in my life. Amen.

Journal

____

____

____

____

____

Day 295

But for the very reason I was shown mercy so that in me, the worst of sinners, Christ Jesus might display his immense patience as an example for those who would believe in him and receive eternal life. Now to the King eternal, immortal, invisible, the only God, be honor and glory for ever and ever. Amen. 1 Timothy 1:16,17

It is interesting, the closer one gets to God, the greater one's sinfulness is felt. Praise God for his forgiveness - he washes away the guilt of sin. See 1 John 1:9.

Prayer: Dear Heavenly Father, I praise, worship and adore you for washing away my sin in the blood of Christ Jesus which he shed on the cross. Thank you for the blood of Christ Jesus which covers me and protects me. Amen.

Journal

____

____

____

____

____

Day 296

Timothy, my son, I am giving you this command in keeping with the prophecies once made about you, so that by recalling them you may fight the battle well, holding on to faith and a good conscience, which some have rejected and so have suffered shipwreck with regard to the faith. Among them are Hymenaeus and Alexander, who I have handed over to satan to be taught not to blaspheme. 1 Timothy 1:18-20

Sadly, some christians backslide, but it does not mean God has given up on them. In this reference, 'turned over to satan' it is thought to mean to be 'out of the sanctuary of the church', hoping for them to repent and be accepted back into fellowship, or, for the prodigal to return. Pray for the prodigals you know.

Prayer: Dear Heavenly Father, I bring you *(name the prodigal)* to you in your precious name. I ask that you prod their heart and mind to think about you and the good things you offer them. Help them to see you above their sin and want to be in relationship with you again. Amen.

Journal

____

____

____

____

____

Day 297

I urge, then, first of all, that petitions, prayers, intercession and thanksgiving be made for all people - for kings and all those in authority, that we may live peaceful and quiet lives in all godliness and holiness. 1 Timothy 2:1,2

The books of 1 and 2 Timothy, and Titus are known as pastoral letters, or, letters written with information to successfully run a church and care for the parishioners. We learn the expected behavior for church members in Paul's writing. The key theme is 'godliness', or living a life which reflects Jesus, his character and his example.

Prayer: Dear Heavenly Father, thank you for your word which is pertinent in each age of old history as well as recent history. You are alpha and omega, and you know the beginning and end with everything in between. I trust you. You are truth, reality and power. Amen.

Journal

____

____

____

____

____

Day 298

This is good, and pleases God our Savior, who wants all people to be saved and to come to a knowledge of the truth. For there is one God and one mediator between God and mankind, the man Christ Jesus, who gave himself as a ransom for all people. This has not been witnessed to at the proper time. 1 Timothy 2:3-6

Salvation is offered to all people, God desires that all of us accept his offer of salvation. Jesus Christ is our Savior, and it is he who stands between us and God, mediating for us. It is his blood which covers the filth of our sin from God's eyes, making us acceptable to God. See Hebrews 4:14-16, 5:1-10. Jesus is our High Priest, our mediator between God and man.

Prayer: Dear Heavenly Father, Your plan of salvation is so perfect. You sent Jesus to become a man so he will be an example to show me how to live my life the way you planned for me. Not only that, since he has been a man, he is able to empathize with me and intercede before the throne of grace for me. O how wonderful you are and I am eternally grateful for your perfect plan of salvation, and your lavish love toward me. Amen.

Journal

Day 299

And for this purpose I was appointed a herald and an apostle - I am telling the truth, I am not lying - and a true and faithful teacher of the Gentiles. Therefore, I want the men everywhere to pray, lifting up holy hands without anger or disputing. 1 Timothy 2:7,8

Paul is stating that he was appointed the herald, or authoritative announcer, to proclaim the works of salvation to the Gentiles. He continues his letter by asking men and women to pray together and to leave their anger and arguments behind.

Prayer: Dear Heavenly Father, I love the unity you bring to your family. Thank you that you showed us how to live in love and harmony when you were on this earth. Help me to choose unity in my relationships with others. Amen.

Journal

____

____

____

____

____

Day 300

I also want the women to dress modestly, with decency and propriety, adorning themselves, not with elaborate hairstyles or gold or pearls or expensive clothes, but with good deeds, appropriate for women who profess to worship God. 1 Timothy 2:9,10

In the society where Paul and Timothy were living, luxury and personal beauty/pleasant appearances were put on display. Here Paul is cautioning Timothy and his church to exhibit good deeds, love, kindness, and a godly life from the inside out. Each of us at some time has seen or has been drawn into the phenomenon of a 'valley girl/guy' complex, or 'keeping up with the Joneses', and the feeling of being pressed into competing or conforming with each other regarding our appearance, or professional/economic status. Paul is suggesting for women to present themselves with moderate adornment, and to express their love for each other with good deeds - e.g., helping the poor, caring for widows and orphans, and serving God with a loving and caring heart.

Prayer: Dear Heavenly Father, I want to be the one who shines for you from the inside out, and not to be showy in my appearance or attitude. Keep me humble and loving to others through the love you give to me. Thank you. Amen.

Journal

____

____

____

____

____

Day 301

A woman should learn in quietness and full submission. I do not permit a woman to teach or assume authority over a man; she must be quiet. For Adam was formed first, then Eve. 1 Timothy 2:11-13

There are many thoughts about this passage. Some scholars think that Paul is suggesting to prohibit untrained women from teaching. Others suggest that Paul did not allow a woman to be an official teacher in the church. However, women have a history in Christendom and have held positions for furthering the Gospel of Christ Jesus. Many were martyred. Nowadays we have Pastoras in matriarchal countries, Deaconesses in our churches, Women's Ministries in our churches, Parachurch Women's Ministries - e.g., Beth Moore, Joy Meyers, and more, who are making a mark for Jesus.

Prayer: Dear Heavenly Father, I am available to do your will. Stir my heart to hear your voice which says, 'This is the way, walk in it with me.' Amen.

Journal

____

____

____

____

____

Day 302

And Adam was not the one deceived; it was the woman who was deceived and became a sinner. But women will be saved through childbearing - if they continue in faith, love and holiness with propriety. 1 Timothy 2:14,15

Interesting to note that the blame of the fall often focuses on Eve, but did you notice Adam fell too - he could have said to Eve, 'No! as your protector, 'stop', but he didn't. Or, he could have called out to God for help, but he didn't. He was 'sucked in' as well. Pray for strength to not be 'sucked' into the temptations of the world.

Prayer: Dear Heavenly Father, Keep me strong and true to you, especially in the midst of temptation, or difficult times. I trust you always, and place my hand in yours, knowing you will never leave me, nor forsake me. Amen.

Journal

Day 303

Here is a trustworthy saying: Whoever aspires to be an overseer desires a noble task. Now the overseer is to be above reproach, faithful to his wife, temperate, self-controlled, respectable, hospitable, able to teach... 1 Timothy 3:1,2

The word 'overseer' is a similar word as 'elder' in our present-day context. Paul continues to describe the morals and character which is expected from a church elder, which continues in tomorrow's verses. Paul also rules out polygamy and adultery in the list of expectations.

Prayer: Dear Heavenly Father, Thank you for describing your wishes in your word so we can understand your expectations. I pray for the overseers in my church and ask that you draw them to you to live a life of Godly love and respect to you and to those around them. Amen.

Journal

____

____

____

____

____

Day 304

…not given to drunkenness, not violent but gentle, not quarrelsome, not a lover of money. He must manage his own family well and see that his children obey him, and he must do so in a manner worthy of full respect. 1 Timothy 3:3,4

The list of the 'overseer' or elder expectations continues to rule out bad behavior and to tackle family relationships - suggesting that if a man cannot manage himself or his family, how could he manage or 'oversee' a church? Makes a heap of sense, doesn't it? The list does tend to question our behavior as well. How would you measure up, if you were considered to be an overseer or an overseer's wife, or a deacon/deaconess?

Prayer: Dear Heavenly Father, Oh lord, how do I measure up. I choose to be the one who loves my immediate family and my christian family. I choose to not quarrel with folk, and ask that you give me direction as to the management of my feelings when I want to be quarrelsome, or angry. I trust you Lord. Amen.

Journal

____

____

____

____

____

Day 305

(If anyone does not know how to manage his own family, how can he take care of God's church?) He must not be a recent convert, or he may become conceited and fall under the same judgment as the devil. He must also have a good reputation with outsiders, so that he will not fall into disgrace and into the devil's trap. 1 Timothy 3:5-7

These words of advice speak for themselves don't they? And, they are pertinent for today's church management, and the management of each of our own lives.

Prayer: Dear Heavenly Father, I ask you to keep me honest and transparent before you and before others in my day to day life. Thank you. Amen.

Journal

____

____

____

____

____

Day 306

In the same way, deacons are to be worthy of respect, sincere, not indulging in much wine, and not pursuing dishonest gain. They must keep hold of the deep truths of the faith with a clear conscience. They must first be tested and then if there is nothing against them, let them serve as deacons. 1 Timothy 3:8-10

Deacons and deaconesses are servers in the church. They are meant to be available to help with the physical upkeep, behind the scenes work of the church, much like a caretaker and servant. Since they represent the church, their character must also be Christlike. Do you enjoy serving in your church? List the activities you are involved in, pray over others which the Lord has placed on your heart.

Prayer: Dear Heavenly Father, Thank you for giving me *(name the tasks)* to perform within your body. I enjoy serving you and others. I ask you give me strength, perception, honesty, and a loving heart as I serve you. Amen.

Journal

____

____

____

____

____

Day 307

In the same way, the women are to be worthy of respect, not malicious talkers but temperate and trustworthy in everything. 1 Timothy 3:11

Paul's reference to 'the women', could refer to a deaconess, a deacon's wife, or the pastor's wife. However, it could mean all of them as a pastor's wife, a deacon's wife and a deaconess are all expected to be above reproof.

Prayer: Dear Heavenly Father, Today I pray for the men and women in my church leadership. I pray for (NAME THE MEN AND WOMEN) and ask for you to give them strength, guidance, power, faith and love, to enable them to serve your body in accordance to your word. Amen.

Journal

____

____

____

____

____

Day 308

A deacon must be faithful to his wife and must manage his children and his household well. Those who have served well gain an excellent standing and great assurance in their faith in Christ Jesus. 1 Timothy 3:12,13

These verses could indicate the household to also include servants and/or slaves. To put it into current perspective, i.e., in a present day family, it would mean all those living under the same roof. Our Lord blesses those who obey him and follow his lead - who represent him at home and outside the home. May we be found representing our Lord in all we do, behind doors and publicly.

Prayer: Dear Heavenly Father, Keep me true to you, Lord Jesus. Give me strength to shine my light brightly in this sad, dark world. Amen.

Journal

____

____

____

____

____

Day 309

Although I hope to come to you soon, I am writing you these instructions so that, if I am delayed, you will know how people ought to conduct themselves in God's household, which is the church of the Living God, the pillar and foundation of the truth. 1 Timothy 3:14,15

Interesting how Paul talks about the church as 'God's household'. It alters the picture or concept as to how most of us see church…. comparing it to a household, which has protections, securities, sustenance, rules, expected behaviors and generations. How does your church look as a household? Note your thoughts in your Journal.

Prayer: Dear Heavenly Father, thank you for my family, both biological and spiritual. Thank you for the security of being in your family, and the protections that it provides. I pray for discernment and guidance to use the gifts and talents you have provided me, in order to further the gospel, to grow into your likeness in myself and to help others to grow into your likeness as well.

Journal

____

____

____

____

____

Day 310

Beyond all question, the mystery from which true godliness springs is great: He appeared in the flesh, was vindicated by the Spirit, was seen by angels, was preached among the nations, was believed on in the world, was taken up in glory. 1 Timothy 3:16

This is the same Jesus who rescued us from sin and lives in us by the Holy Spirit. Here is the mystery - a Holy God becomes our savior to redeem us from sin, to rise again proving he was divine, ascended back into heaven, then sending his Holy Spirit to be with us as a helper/ supporter/power-giver, so we can be transformed to become more like him, and at the end of our lives, to live with him in heaven. Praise his holy name.

Prayer: Dear Heavenly Father, What can I say? Hallelujah, Hallelujah, Hallelujah. You paid it all, you rescued me, I am in your arms, I am humbly enamored by your love. Hallelujah. Amen.

Journal

____

____

____

____

____

Day 311

The Spirit clearly says that in later times some will abandon the faith and follow deceiving spirits and things taught by demons. Such teachings come through hypocritical liars, whose consciences have been seared as with a hot iron. I Timothy 4:1,2

Wow, what an expression, 'seared with a hot iron'. When we sear our meat, the heat closes of the blood or lymph vessels to prevent seepage of the fluids and keeps the meat moist. Here, Paul is referring to the conscience being closed. Oh how we need to keep our conscience open to the guiding voice of the Holy Spirit, in each of our days.

Prayer: Dear Heavenly Father, I choose to hear you. Show me your ways, Oh Lord, teach me your paths, so that I will follow your footsteps in this life. Amen.

Journal

____
____
____
____
____

Day 312

They forbid people to marry and order them to abstain from certain foods, which God created to be received with thanksgiving by those who believe and who know the truth. For everything God created is good, and nothing is to be rejected if it is received with thanksgiving, because it is consecrated by the word of God and prayer. 1 Timothy 4:3,5

Gnosticism was one of the heresies which the early church grappled with. Acetism is the central belief of the Gnostic heresy. It believes that the material world is evil. Another concept Paul brings up is thankfulness for our food. Do you say 'grace' before you eat? What do you say? Do you pray out loud or in your heart? Journal your response.

Prayer: Dear Heavenly Father, thank you for your many daily blessings. Thank you for my food, my place of rest, my comfortable bed, the clothes you provide for me through my wage or other method of income. Thank you for my home. I don't want to take them for granted and acknowledge your hand in your provision for me. Amen.

Journal

____

____

____

____

____

Day 313

If you point these things out to the brothers and sisters, you will be a good minister of Christ Jesus, nourished on the truths of the faith and of the good teaching that you have followed. Have nothing to do with godless myths and old wives tales; rather, train yourself to be godly. For physical training is of some value, but godliness has value for all things, holding promise for both the present life and the life to come. 1 Timothy 4:6-8

Paul is placing godliness training at a higher value than physical training. The reason is because it lasts for eternity - whereas physical training is finite. May we concentrate on the issues and truth that matters eternally in our lives and the lives of others.

Song: Today, sing the old song - Turn your eyes upon Jesus, Look full in his wonderful face, and the things of this earth will grow strangely dim, in the light of his glory and grace. Amen.

Journal

____

____

____

____

____

Day 314

This is a trustworthy saying that deserves full acceptance. That is why we labor and strive, because we have put our hope in the living God, who is the Savior of all people, and especially of those who believe. 1 Timothy 4:9,10

Hebrews 11:1 states, 'Now faith is being sure of what we hope for and certain of what we do not see.' Our hope is in Christ, the salvation he offers, the adventuresome life he has planned for us and for eternal life. Without him we are lost! Our God is living - he is alpha and omega - the beginning and the end, though, the Bible tells us there is no end - which also is the meaning of eternity.

Prayer: Dear Heavenly Father, How I trust you and place my very being in your hand. I hope in you, I trust you, I live for you. Thank you that you see me and know my name. Amen.

Journal

____

____

____

____

____

Day 315

Command and teach these things. Don't let anyone look down on you because you are young, but set an example for the believers in speech, in conduct, in love, in faith and purity. Until I come, devote yourself to the public reading of Scripture, to preaching and to teaching. Do not neglect your gift, which was given you through prophecy when the body of elders laid their hands on you. 1 Timothy 4:11-14

These words are for you today - set an example in speech, life, love, faith and purity. This sad world needs people to live wholesomely with good morals and genuine kindness. Let that be your prayer today.

Prayer: Dear Heavenly Father, May my life show 'You in Me'. May I be that beacon of light for you, showing others a life of good morals and genuine kindness. Show me today where I can deliver random acts of kindness to people who need you. Amen.

Journal

____
____
____
____
____

Day 316

Be diligent in these matters: give yourself wholly to them, so that everyone may see your progress. Watch your life and doctrine closely. Persevere in then, because if you do, you will save both yourself and your hearers. 1 Timothy 4:15,16

God uses his people, his body, to be instruments of hope and salvation to hurting people in this sad, sinful world. He uses us to sow seeds for him to water, grow and harvest. Our Lord has placed us on this earth to be his instrument - an instrument of peace, joy, love, generosity, kindness, an example to lead others to a saving knowledge of the savior of mankind - Christ Jesus. Today, spend time contemplating and praising God for all he has done for you. Journal your joys and answers to prayer.

Prayer: Dear Heavenly Father, I praise you for your perfect plan for me. You made me intricately for the work you have planned for my life. You are amazing and awesome, you reign in heaven above, in wisdom, power and love. I humbly bow before you and worship you. Amen.

Journal

____

____

____

____

Day 317

Do not rebuke an older man harshly but exhort him as if he were your father. Treat younger men as brothers, older women as mothers, and younger women as sisters, with absolute purity. 1 Timothy 5:1,2

Sage advice to a young pastor starting out in his first pastorate. Also, sage advice to us all in our relationships with one another. Jesus tells us to love our neighbor as ourselves - Luke 10:27. This means preferring our neighbor at the same level we prefer ourselves. Who is your neighbor? Spend time Journaling your neighbor's names and make a plan to pray for each one.

Prayer: Dear Heavenly Father, Today I pray for *(name your neighbors)*, and ask that you will move in their lives so they can hear you and respond to you. Use me to be a seed sower in their lives, so that they become aware of you and want you in their lives. Amen.

Journal

____

____

____

____

____

Day 318

Give proper recognition to those widows who are really in need. But if a widow has children or grandchildren, these should learn first of all to put their religion into practice by caring for their own family and so repaying their parents and grandparents, for this is pleasing to God. 1 Timothy 5:3,4

Widows were particularly vulnerable in ancient societies, because pensions, government assistance, life insurance, and the like, were not available to them as we have them in our society. Plus, to put this scripture into present day context, it could include single parenting with children at home, refugees, elderly, and homelessness. How do you see this scripture outworked in your life? Journal your thoughts and pray over your ideas.

Prayer: Dear Heavenly Father, I appreciate you caring for me and my loved ones. Thank you for *(name your ideas)* and thank you for your provisions which are new and fresh to me each day. Amen.

Journal

____
____
____
____
____

Day 319

The widow who is really in need and left all alone puts her hope in God and continues night and day to pray and to ask God for help. But the widow who lives for pleasure is dead even while she lives. Give the people these instructions, so that no one may be open to blame. Anyone who does not provide for their relatives, and especially for their own household, has denied the faith and is worse than an unbeliever. 1 Timothy 5:5-8

Paul is pointing out that a wanton widow is spiritually dead. He is also reminding Timothy to remind his congregation of their social and familial obligations in caring and providing for their families.

Prayer: Dear Heavenly Father, I do not want to be amiss in caring for my family. Help me to care for *(name family members, even if some are estranged)*. Show me how to love on the ones who are unlovely, in your name. Give me grace to be your eyes, your ears, your hands and your feet toward my family. Amen.

Journal

____

____

____

____

Day 320

No widow may be put on the list of widows unless she is over sixty, has been faithful to her husband and is well known for her good deeds, such as bringing up her children, showing hospitality, washing the feet of the Lord's people, helping those in trouble and devoting herself to all kinds of good deeds. 1 Timothy 5:9,10

It appears that the church in Ephesus has a list of widows. Paul describes the conditions and expectations of the character of widows on the list. She seems comparable to the Virtuous Woman in Proverbs 31:10-31. Today, do some self-reflection using the characteristics Paul mentions - Journal and pray over your discoveries.

Prayer: Dear Heavenly Father, I want to shine for you in my life. Help me to develop the characteristics of faithfulness to you, my family, my friends, and my acquaintances. Give me strength to face hard discoveries about myself, and give me strength to rely on you to develop Godly character in my life. Amen.

Journal

____

____

____

____

____

Day 321

As for the younger widows, do not put them on such a list. For when their sensual desires overcome their dedication to Christ, they want to marry. Thus, they bring judgment on themselves, because they have broken their first pledge. 1 Timothy 5:11,12

There are varying thoughts about the meaning of these verses. Some scholars think that if a widow was placed on the list, she pledged devotion to Christ which would be compromised if she were to marry. Or, if the widow married outside the christian faith, her dedication would also be compromised.

Prayer: Dear Heavenly Father, I pray for *(name those you know who are single or widowed)*, and ask you that you would give them acceptance, peace and joy in their singleness or widowhood. Amen.

Journal

____

____

____

____

____

Day 322

Besides, they get into the habit of being idle and going about from house to house. And not only do they become idlers, but also busybodies who talk nonsense, saying things they ought not to. So, I counsel younger widows to marry, to have children, to manage their homes and to give the enemy no opportunity for slander. Some have in fact already turned away to follow satan. 1 Timothy 5:13-15

Hard words, but truthful concepts. Even though we may not be widows, or maybe we are single - let us guard ourselves from gossip, busy bodying and idleness. May our words be like 'apples of gold in settings of silver' - Proverbs 25:11. May our heart be open to speak gracious words of kindness, gentleness, peace, love and joy.

Prayer: Dear Heavenly Father, I give you my heart, my mind and my lips, so that I may speak words of truth in love, and words of kindness with the attitude of gentleness, peace, love and joy. Amen.

Journal

____

____

____

____

Day 323

If any woman who is a believer has widows in her care, she should continue to help them and not let the church be burdened with them, so that the church can help those widows who are really in need. 1 Timothy 5:16

Extended family living is so healthy and helpful if it functions properly. Many cultures adhere to this practice - it is the westernized families who are more nuclear, single, blended in structure, which often rules out the mixed generations all living under one roof or in close proximity. What is your family structure. Journal how your family cares for each other. Pray for your family members today.

Prayer: Dear Heavenly Father, I pray for *(name your family members)* again today. I ask that you will give us the desire to live our lives in unity, honesty, faith and consideration toward each other. Help us to be mindful of each other's boundaries and respect them. Amen.

Journal

____

____

____

____

____

Day 324

The elders who direct the affairs of the church well are worthy of double honor, especially those whose work is preaching and teaching. For Scripture says, 'Do not muzzle an ox while it is treading out the grain,' and, 'the worker deserves his wages'. 1 Timothy 5:17,18

Paul is stating that respect is due to those who honestly work toward the 'equipping (preparing) the saints' - Ephesians 4:12. Those who have an honest, selfless attitude, who are in the service for our Lord. Often it is easy to take for granted those who are serving the Lord and take from them without gratitude or an attitude of respect.

Prayer: Dear Heavenly Father, I pray for the elders and leaders of my church. *(Name your church elders and leaders)*. Keep them in your will, helping them to hear your voice and provide honest leadership as they lead your body. Cover them with your precious blood, and keep them from the temptations and deceptions from the enemy. Amen.

Journal

Day 325

Do not entertain an accusation against an elder unless it is brought by two or three witnesses. But those elders who are sinning you are to reprove before everyone, so that the others may take warning. 1 Timothy 5:19,20

Recent history has seen many public accusations about prominent christian leaders who have fallen into sin, most commonly, immorality. Today, pray for the leaders at your place of worship, for the Lord to keep them from the pride of their position and success, and the lust of the flesh (immorality), and riches, fame or popularity. Ask the Lord to guide them into all truth, to be faithful to their wife and family.

Prayer: Dear Heavenly Father, I pray for the leaders at my church, for you to keep them from the pride of their position and success, and the lust of the flesh (immorality), and riches, fame or popularity. I ask you to guide them into all truth, to be faithful to their wife and family. Amen.

Journal

____

____

____

____

____

Day 326

I charge you, in the sight of God and Christ Jesus and the elect angels, to keep these instructions without partiality, and to do nothing out of favoritism. Do not be hasty in the laying on of hands, and do not share in the sins of others. Keep yourself pure. 1 Timothy 5:21,22

Paul is charging Timothy, in God's sight and in the sight of his angels, to keep the instructions he has written in this letter. In essence and where pertinent, the meaning of the instructions are for us as well - to care for those in need, mind your mouth, live an honorable, moral and Godly life. Don't follow those who favor others, don't be partial. All in all, live a life which is pleasing to Jesus Christ - following the example he set.

Prayer: Dear Heavenly Father, I choose to live a life which honors you. Help me to mind my mouth, and to live honorably and morally for you. Keep me in a place where I care for others, so I will not choose one over another. I choose to love others as you have loved me. Thank you. Amen.

Journal

____

____

____

____

____

Day 327

Stop drinking only water, and use a little wine because of your stomach and your frequent illnesses. The sins of some are obvious, reaching the place of judgment ahead of them; the sins of others trail behind them. In the same way, good deeds are obvious, and even those that are not obvious cannot remain hidden forever. 1 Timothy 5:23-25

Timothy must have had stomach ailments, and Paul is recommending he drinks a little wine to soothe the problem. Or, maybe, it was difficult to find safe drinking water in his location of residence, and wine was safer to drink instead of water. Paul finishes this part of his letter to assure Timothy to be aware of the hidden sins of those around him as well as see their good deeds. Today, do a little introspection to identify hidden sins, and also good deeds in your life.

Prayer: Dear Heavenly Father, Give me strength to stand strong for you. Open my heart and mind to areas which need a little work, so I may grow to be more like you. Amen.

Journal

____

____

____

____

____

Day 328

All who are under the yoke of slavery should consider their masters worthy of full respect, so that God's name and our teaching may not be slandered. Those who have believing masters should not show them disrespect just because they are fellow believers. Instead, they should serve them even better because their masters are dear to them as fellow believers and are devoted to the welfare of their slaves. These are the things you are to teach and insist on. 1 Timothy 6:1,2

Even though we are not slaves or masters of slaves, we could consider this advice to be appropriate for our employment and employer, or the student-teacher relationship. Whatever situation you may be in, be cognizant of your relationship with Jesus, and live your life following his example.

Memorize Proverbs 3:5,6 'Trust in the Lord with all your heart and lean not on your own understanding; in all your ways submit to him, and he will make your paths straight.'

Journal

____

____

____

____

____

Day 329

If anyone teaches otherwise and does not agree to the sound instruction of our Lord Jesus Christ and to godly teaching, they are conceited and understand nothing. They have an unhealthy interest in controversies and quarrels about words that result in envy, strife, malicious talk, evil suspicions and constant friction between people of corrupt mind, who have been robbed of the truth and who think that godliness is a means to financial gain. 1 Timothy 6:3,5

Beware of these people Paul describes - they are found in the church as gossipers, power strugglers, those trying to please the leaders so to promote themselves. Let you be found trustworthy and faithful in doing the work of the Lord with a humble manner.

Prayer: Dear Heavenly Father, may I be found faithful. May I be found listening to you, my Lord, and following your lead, and not the lead of my own selfish desires. I choose you. Amen.

Journal

____

____

____

____

____

Day 330

But godliness with contentment is great gain. For we brought nothing into the world, and we can take nothing out of it. But if we have food and clothing, will we be content with that? 1 Timothy 6:6-8

Choose this route which Paul describes for our great gain in the Lord - choose godliness. How does godliness look? Here are some verses which help to see what Godliness looks like; a humble and contrite spirit (Psalm 51:17), evidencing the fruit of the spirit (Gal 5:21,22), found doing God's work with the love of the Lord, such as, getting involved in service, standing for righteousness and justice, loving your family and caring for God's family through generosity and hospitality.

Prayer: Dear Heavenly Father, make me a vessel of your peace. Make me a vessel to show mercy. Make me a vessel which evidences the fruit of your spirit. Amen.

Journal

____

____

____

____

____

Day 331

Those who want to get rich fall into temptation and a trap and into many foolish and harmful desires that plunge people into ruin and destruction. For the love of money is a root of all kinds of evil. Some people, eager for money, have wandered from the faith and pierced themselves with many griefs. 1 Timothy 6:9,10

How true is this. You can see the truth of Paul's words in the life of many celebrities, e.g., Elvis Presley who started off as a gospel singer - then he succumbed to fame - there are so many more whom you can research. Keep your eyes on Jesus, he is the one who blesses us.

Prayer: Dear Heavenly Father, I turn my eyes on you, Jesus, I look to your fullness and grace, and I want the things of this world to grow dim, as I grow to be more like you. Amen.

Journal

____

____

____

____

____

Day 332

But you, man of God, flee from all this, and pursue righteousness, godliness, faith, love, endurance and gentleness. Fight the good fight of the faith. Take hold of the eternal life to which you were called when you made your good confession in the presence of many witnesses. 1 Timothy 6:11,12

Let this advice from Paul to Timothy also be from Paul to you and me. Focus our days, hours and minutes on Jesus - what would Jesus have me do? Let his love, peace and joy permeate your being and shine through you to others. May this be your prayer today.

Prayer: Dear Heavenly Father, let your love, peace and joy permeate my being today, that you will shine through me today, to a hurting world. Amen.

Journal

____

____

____

____

____

Day 333

In the sight of God, who gives life to everything, and of Christ Jesus, who while testifying before Pontius Pilate made the good confession, I charge you to keep this command without spot or blame until the appearing of our Lord Jesus Christ,...... 1 Timothy 6:13,14

The command Paul refers to is in verses 11 and 12 - yesterday's reading. However, today let's think about the stanza, 'in the sight of God.' God is everywhere in this world through his creation and in us through his Holy Spirit. We cannot hide anything from God because he is all knowing. We are free to be honest with him - he knows our weaknesses and strengths, anyway. He loves you and he made you - praise Him for the freedom he gives to you.

Prayer: Dear Heavenly Father, I find peace, safety and joy knowing that I do not need to hide anything from you. You know anyway, and I feel safe talking to you about what is on my mind, what I did or am thinking about. Thank you for not throwing me away because of my humanness - you love me anyway. Amen.

Journal

Day 334

....which God will bring about in his own time - God, the blessed and only Ruler, the King of kings and Lord of lords, who alone is immortal and who lives in unapproachable light, whom no one has seen or can see. To him be honor and might forever. Amen. 1 Timothy 6:15,16

This is a beautiful description of our Lord and God. Also see Revelation 4 for a glimpse into God's throne room. With an open heart and your arms stretched out to heaven, sing praises to him and worship the Lord today. Tell him how you love him and are desperate for him. Thank him for his plan of redemption and that he included you in his plan. Honor and praise him in all that you do.

Sing the song: I love you Lord, and I lift my voice, to worship you, Oh my Lord, Rejoice, in what you hear, Let me be a sweet, sweet sound in your ear. Singing hallelujah, hallelujah, praise and worship to the King. Amen.

Journal

____

____

____

____

____

Day 335

Command those who are rich in this present world not to be arrogant nor to put their hope in wealth, which is so uncertain, but to put their hope in God, who richly provides us with everything for our enjoyment. 1 Timothy 6:17

Sometimes personal riches and successes can blind a person's spiritual eyes, from where and how he or she got the riches and success in the first place. God is the one who gives and takes away - or, allows it to happen. We are encouraged to always look to the Lord for our daily needs and forgiveness of our sins. Keep your eyes on Jesus and not the things which surround you.

Prayer: Dear Heavenly Father, I look to you for my needs. Thank you for your abundant provisions to me each day. I thank you for *(name what He has provided for you)*, and praise you for your faithfulness to me each day. Amen.

Journal

____

____

____

____

____

Day 336

Command them to do good, to be rich in good deeds, and to be generous and willing to share. In this way they will lay up treasure for themselves as a firm foundation for the coming age, so that they may take hold of the life that is truly life. 1 Timothy 6:18,19

When God blesses us, he wants us to pass the blessings on to others. Have you considered that the Lord may bless you with riches so that you can pass those riches on to others? Today, in your quiet time, consider what the Lord has blessed you with, through which he may be asking you to bless those around you, or provide for specific needs.

Prayer: Dear Heavenly Father, you delight in blessing your children. Thank you for your blessings toward me. Thank you for *(NAME THE ONES WHICH COME TO MIND)*. I choose to share your blessings with others. Open my heart and mind to see and hear your gentle prompting. Amen.

Journal

Day 337

Timothy, guard what has been entrusted to your care. Turn away from godless chatter and the opposing ideas of what is falsely called knowledge, which some have professed and in so doing have departed from the faith. Grace be with you all. 1 Timothy 6: 20,21

Apt words of advise in our current social and political context today. Yes, there is so much information out there which is called 'knowledge', but does it draw a person toward faith, or, pull a person away from the faith? One example is the philosophy of humanism and all the theories which have grown out of it.

Prayer: Dear Heavenly Father, I ask for you to help me to keep my mind and heart on the truth of your word and keep them resonating within my being and my focus on you. Amen.

Journal

____
____
____
____
____

Day 338

Paul, an apostle of Christ Jesus by the will of God, in keeping with the promise of life that is in Christ Jesus, To Timothy, my dear son; Grace, mercy and peace from God the Father and Christ Jesus our Lord. 2 Timothy 1:1,2

Paul always has a caring greeting and salutation in his letters - this helps us see his love and respect for the readers and recipients. He reminds Timothy that he, Paul, is an apostle - one called and sent by God, and he sends him grace, mercy and peace from God. Now - do you realize that God also sends you grace, mercy and peace? Think about this amazing gesture throughout your day to day and pray that each of those gifts may permeate through you - in your speech and actions, as your day progresses. Praise him for his goodness to you.

Prayer: Dear Heavenly Father, You are so good to me. I love your peace, mercy and blessing which are new to me each morning. May you permeate through me in my speech and actions throughout today. You are good. Amen.

Journal

____

____

____

____

____

Day 339

I thank God, whom I serve, as my ancestors did, with a clear conscience, as night and day I constantly remember you in my prayers. Recalling your tears, I long to see you, so that I may be filled with joy. 2 Timothy 1:3,4

Paul knows his life was nearly at an end, and he was lonely in the cold dungeon where he was imprisoned. He wanted Timothy to join him. Today we will concentrate on his words, 'clear conscience'. In your life, how does it relate to your relationship with Jesus? Jesus is present with you always in the form of the Holy Spirit - there is no reason to hide anything from him - he knows anyway. Today, have an honest talk with Jesus about the things which bother you.

Prayer: Dear Heavenly Father, I want to talk to you about *(name the items)*. You know anyway, so I don't hide it from you, but, instead, to talk honestly to you about it. *(state what you want to lay open before the Lord)*. Help me to see your hand and feel your presence in my life. Amen.

Journal

____

____

____

____

____

Day 340

I am reminded of your sincere faith, which first lived in your grandmother Lois and in your mother Eunice and, I am persuaded, now lives in you also. For this reason I remind you to fan into flame the gift of God, which is in you through the laying on of my hands. 1 Timothy 1:5,6

It is interesting to note that Godly gifts are not given to us in its full entirety, they are to be grown and developed in us through use. Today, concentrate on the gifts which God has given you - See 1 Corinthians 12. List the gifts you see in your life, ask the Lord to use you in each of them. Look for the opportunities you are given. Talk to a respected christian about them - pray together. Rest in the Lord and thank him for all he has given you.

Prayer: Dear Heavenly Father, thank you for the gifts of *(name the gifts)* you have placed in my life. Help me to use them to your benefit and according to your will. Thank you for your great mercies and love you lavish on me each day. Amen.

Journal

____

____

____

____

____

Day 341

For the Spirit God gave us does not make us timid, but gives us power, love and self-discipline. 2 Timothy 1:7

Even though Paul is referring to Timothy's apparent lack of confidence, this verse is so apt for each of us today. Have you ever needed self-discipline? Well, this verse states it straight - God has given us the power of self-discipline. It is also one of the fruit of the Spirit - see Galatians 5:23. Amazing. How much do you believe this for your situation(s)? Can you trust God for his full power in your life? If so, what does it look like? If not, what needs to happen for you to realize it in your life? Journal your thoughts.

Prayer: Dear Heavenly Father, I want you and your promises in my life. I want your power to help me in situations when I am tempted to succumb to a vice which has beset me in the past or is something new. Give me faith and strength to keep me focused on you and your promises. Amen.

Journal

____

____

____

____

Day 342

So do not be ashamed of the testimony about our Lord or of me his prisoner. Rather, join with me in suffering for the gospel, by the power of God. He has saved us and called us to a holy life - not because of anything we have done but because of his own purpose and grace. 2 Timothy 1:8,9a

Paul encourages Timothy to continue the work of service to the Lord and to enter into the suffering for the gospel as he has done. Always there has been persecution toward those who truly believe, have faith in God, and live a holy life - the devil hates it! Be on alert and faithful to your belief and commitment to our Lord Jesus Christ.

Also, did you notice that we have been saved, not because of anything we have done, but because of his own purpose and grace. Two powerful concepts to ponder today.

Prayer: Dear Heavenly Father, thank you for your grace and mercy toward me, as a free gift because you wanted me to be yours. I accept. Keep me strong and true to you in my daily walk through this journey of life. Thank you. Amen.

Journal

____
____
____
____
____

Day 343

This grace was given us in Christ Jesus before the beginning of time, but it has now been revealed through the appearing of our Savior, Christ Jesus, who has destroyed death and has brought life and immortality to light through the gospel.

2 Timothy 1:9b,10

These powerful verses are sustenance to a christian - eternal grace, our savior destroyed death, our savior has bought us light through the gospel. Gospel means: God Offers Sinful People Eternal Life - good news! Our savior is Jesus - who is part of the Godhead. He is Alpha and Omega - ever powerful and all knowing. Love on him and purposefully look for ways to serve him today.

Prayer: Dear Heavenly Father, You are an awesome God who lavishes your love on me. I choose you too. Thank you for destroying the power of sin and death and giving us salvation through the gospel. Show me was I can serve you better today. Amen.

Journal

____

____

____

____

____

Day 344

And of this gospel I was appointed a herald and an apostle and a teacher. That is why I am suffering as I am. Yet this is no cause for shame, because I know whom I have believed, and am convinced that he is able to guard what I have entrusted to him until that day. 2 Timothy 1:11,12

Paul is confident that his service for the Lord and the gospel he and his co-workers taught and spread was and is honest and truthful and he would have live it, teach it and spread it to the end of his days. He is confident in the reality of God through Christ Jesus and the life and message Christ Jesus came to proclaim. He provides us a wonderful example of mankind working in conjunction with the Holy Spirit.

Prayer: Dear Heavenly Father, You are the one whom I believe and am persuaded to spread the good news of salvation to those around me who do not know. May I be your eyes, ears, hands and feet today, to see, hear and attend to those whom I meet in my daily routines. Amen.

Journal

____
____
____
____
____

Day 345

What you heard from me, keep as the pattern of sound teaching, with faith and love in Christ Jesus. Guard the good deposit that was entrusted to you - guard it with the help of the Holy Spirit who lives in us. 2 Timothy 1:13,14

Paul's fatherly advice to Timothy is very apt for you and me in our present circumstances. Keep the word of God and its instructions as a pattern for your life, and guard the truth as you live it, with the help and power of the Holy Spirit, who lives in us.

Memorize Psalm 119:105 'Your word is a lamp for my feet, a light on my path.

Journal

____

____

____

____

Day 346

You know that everyone in the province of Asia has deserted me, including Phygelus and Hermogenes. May the Lord show mercy to the household of Onesiphorus, because he often refreshed me and was not ashamed of my chains. On the contrary, when he was in Rome, he searched hard for me until he found me. May the Lord grant that he will find mercy from the Lord on that day! You know very well in how many ways he helped me in Ephesus. 2 Timothy 1:15-18

Friends can be faithful or selfish. It seems that Paul had both kind, as we do. Pray for your friends today and thank the Lord they are in your life. Develop a deeper friendship with Jesus.

Prayer: Dear Heavenly Father, I pray for *(name your friends)* today, and ask that you draw them closer to you, that they will keep their mind and heart open to hear your still small voice saying, 'this is the way, walk this way.' Amen

Journal

____
____
____
____
____

Day 347

You then, my son, be strong in the grace that is in Christ Jesus. And the things you have heard me say in the presence of many witnesses entrust to reliable people who will also be qualified to teach others. 2 Timothy 2:1,2

Encouragement and instruction from a spiritual father to a spiritual son. It is a healthy way of life to be surrounded by reliable men and women, whom you trust and who impart wisdom and goodness into your life. In your Journal, list the reliable friends or acquaintances you mix with.

Prayer: Dear Heavenly Father, I continue to pray for *(name your friends)*. Please encourage them and support them and open their hearts so they can see you and will want you. Amen.

Journal

____

____

____

____

____

Day 348

Join with me in suffering, like a good soldier of Christ Jesus. No one serving as a soldier gets entangled in civilian affairs, but rather tries to please his commanding officer. Similarly, anyone who competes as an athlete does not receive the victor's crown except by competing according to the rules. The hardworking farmer should be the first to receive a share of the crops. Reflect on what I am saying, for the Lord will give you insight into all this. 2 Timothy 2:3-7

The three takeaways in this passage are these: please God, follow his rules and work for him with all of your heart. In these pieces of advice, Paul tells Timothy the Lord will give him guidance and insight. The Lord is also offering to lead and guide you. How do you respond?

Prayer: Dear Heavenly Father, Thank you for your promise to always be near me. Thank you that you hear me when I call on you. Thank you that you fulfill my desires when I call on you. Amen.

Journal

____

____

____

____

Day 349

Remember Jesus Christ, raised from the dead, descended from David. This is my gospel, for which I am suffering even to the point of being chained like a criminal. But God's word is not chained. 2 Timothy 2:8,9

The last sentence is so powerful. Yes, God and his word is not chained, but instead, it is 'living and active. Sharper than any two-edged sword, it penetrates even to dividing the soul and spirit, joints and marrow; it judges the thoughts and attitudes of the heart.' Hebrews 4:12. Praise God for his gift of the living word, the Holy Bible. May you hide Gods word in your heart so that you will not sin against him. Psalm 119:11

Prayer: Dear Heavenly Father, I hide your word in my heart so I can quote it to myself and to the tempter, when he is pursuing me. Keep me strong in your word. Amen.

Journal

____

____

____

____

Day 350

Therefore, I endure everything for the sake of the elect, that they too may obtain the salvation that is in Christ Jesus, with eternal glory. Here is a trustworthy saying: If we died with him, we will also live with him; if we endure, we will also reign with him. If we disown him, he will also disown us; if we are faithless, he remains faithful, for he cannot disown himself. 2 Timothy 2:10-13

Even though we are 'in' the world, we are not 'of' the world. We are sojourners passing through on our way to our reward where Christ is. However, we are susceptible to the human condition and all which life throws toward us. With Jesus by our side we can live for him and spread the lifesaving truths of the gospel. He is always with us, his promise is sure - see Matthew 28:20

Prayer: Dear Heavenly Father,

Journal

____

____

____

____

____

Day 351

Keep reminding God's people of these things. Warn them before God against quarreling about words; it is of no value, and only ruins those who listen. Do your best to present yourself to God as one approved, a worker who does not need to be ashamed and who correctly handles the word of truth. 2 Timothy 2:14,15

These verses allude to the godless heresy of the time - gnosticism. But it also is worthy for us to consider. Be mindful to guard your words, motives and follow the leading of the Holy Spirit and obey God's instruction per the Holy Bible.

Prayer: Dear Heavenly Father, I ask that you guard my mind, my heart, my will, my mouth. May only honest and wholesome thoughts, words and actions come from me. Amen.

Journal

____

____

____

____

Day 352

Avoid godless chatter, because those who indulge in it will become more and more ungodly. Their teaching will spread like gangrene. Among them are Hymenaeus and Philetus, who have departed from the truth. They say that the resurrection has already taken place and they destroy the faith of some. Nevertheless, God's solid foundation stands firm, sealed with this inscription; 'The Lord knows those who are his,' and, 'Everyone who confesses the name of the Lord must turn away from wickedness.' 2 Timothy 2:16-19

We will always have the 'naysayers' and the Conspiracy Theoriest, but God and his word do not change. God's word is always the same.

Sing the hymn - Choose you this day whom you will serve.

Journal

____

____

____

____

____

Day 353

In a large house there are articles not only of gold and silver, but also of wood and clay; some are for special purposes and some for common use. Those who cleanse themselves from the letter will be instruments for special purposes, made holy, useful to the Master and prepared to do any good work. Flee evil desires of youth and pursue righteousness, faith, love and peace, along with those who call on the Lord out of a pure heart. 2 Timothy 2:20-22

This passage circles in on itself. The articles of gold and silver being metaphors for pursuing righteousness, faith, love and peace. May you pursue these strong attributes in your life.

Prayer: Dear Heavenly Father, Set a guard over my mouth, Lord; Keep watch over the door of my lips. Psalm 141:3. Keep me true to you Lord Jesus, that my life will shine out to others for you. Amen.

Journal

____

____

____

____

____

Day 354

Don't have anything to do with foolish and stupid arguments, because you know they produce quarrels. And the Lord's servant must not be quarrelsome but must be kind to everyone, able to teach, not resentful. Opponents must be gently instructed, in the hope that God will grant them repentance leading them to a knowledge of the truth, and that they will come to their senses and escape from the trap of the devil, who has taken them captive to do his will. 2 Timothy 2:23-26

Wow, potent words about the gnostic quarrelers. However, also pertinent for present day pologetics. When you speak out about your faith, present your view in kind, gentle words, without the spar of accusation or resentfulness.

Prayer: Dear Heavenly Father, thank you for the fruit of the Spirit - love, joy, peace, patience, goodness, kindness, faithfulness, gentleness and self-control. Keep me loving on those around me, even though they may challenge me about my faith. Help me to love and care for them and speak words of truth to them. Amen.

Journal

____

____

____

____

____

Day 355

But mark this: There will be terrible times in the last days. People will be lovers of themselves, lovers of money, boastful, proud, abusive, disobedient to their parents, ungrateful, unholy, without love, unforgiving, slanderous, without self-control, brutal, not lovers of the good, treacherous, rash, conceited, lovers of pleasure rather than lovers of God - having a form of godliness but denying its power. Have nothing to do with such people. 2 Timothy 3:1-5

Does this sound like the current news in our present-day world? It does describe our present-day society, doesn't it? We can see these people Paul is describing living everywhere around us. Be mindful of Paul's warning to Timothy and us. ' Have nothing to do with such people, other than to pray for them and to reach out to them with the good news of salvation.

Prayer: Dear Heavenly Father, may I be your eyes and ears, hands and feet to see and hear those in need, and to help them for your names sake. Amen.

Journal

____

____

____

____

____

Day 356

They are the kind who worm their way into homes to gain control over gullible women, who are loaded down with sins and are swayed by all kinds of evil desires, always learning but never able to come to a knowledge of the truth. Just as Jannes and Jambres opposed Moses, so also these teachers oppose the truth. They are men of depraved minds, who, as far as the faith is concerned, are rejected. But they will not get very far because, as in the case of those men, their folly will be clear to everyone. 2 Timothy 3:6-9

Again, heed the warning from Paul in 2 Timothy 3:5 - 'have nothing to do with them.' Yes, if they are presenting a different teaching, stay far from them, don't entertain them with conversation or hospitality. Move out of their reach.

Prayer: Dear Heavenly Father, keep me true to you. You are truth, and your word is true. Remind me of scripture to keep me close to you and not listen to voices which are designed to pull me away from you. Amen.

Journal

____
____
____
____
____

Day 357

You, however, know all about my teaching, my way of life, my purpose, faith, patience, love, endurance, persecutions, sufferings - what kinds of things happened to me in Antioch, Iconium and Lystra, the persecutions I endured. Yet the Lord rescued me from all of them. In fact, everyone who wants to live a godly life in Christ Jesus will be persecuted, while evildoers and impostors will go from bad to worse, deceiving and being deceived. 2 Timothy 3:10-13

Our God is so faithful, powerful and all knowing. <u>He rescues us</u> - as Paul so honestly states. How has the Lord rescued you. 1 Corinthians 10:12 states: 'No temptation has overtaken you except what is common to mankind. And God is faithful; he will not let you be tempted beyond what you can bear. But when you are tempted, he will also provide a way out so that you can endure it.' Again, <u>He rescues us.</u> Today, Journal your thoughts, and praise him.

Prayer: Dear Heavenly Father, I praise you for your presence with me at all times. Thank you that I can call out to you when I am in difficult situations, and you are there. Amen.

Journal

____

____

____

____

____

Day 358

But as for you, continue in what you have learned and have become convinced of, because you know those from whom you learned it, and how from infancy you have known the Holy Scriptures, which are able to make you wise for salvation through faith in Christ Jesus. All scripture is God-breathed and is useful for teaching, rebuking, correcting and training in righteousness, so that the servant of God may be thoroughly equipped for every good work. 2 Timothy 2:14-16

God has blessed us with his word which teaches, rebukes and corrects us in order that we will be fit and faithful workers for the glory of his kingdom. Amen

Memorize 2 Timothy 3:16

Journal

____
____
____
____
____

Day 359

In the presence of God and of Christ Jesus, who will judge the living and the dead, and in view of his appearing and his kingdom, I give you this charge. Preach the word; be prepared in season and out of season; correct, rebuke and encourage - with great patience and careful instruction. 2 Timothy 4:1,2

This is also a charge to us - be prepared to preach/speak the word in and out of any season - or at any time. Aways be looking for opportunities to preach/speak the gospel - at work, school, in the parking lot, when you are with neighbors - anytime.

Prayer: Dear Heavenly Father, I pray that you will burden my heart for the lost and/or floundering. I choose to speak up for you and share your good news through the way I live my life and what I say. Amen.

Journal

____

____

____

____

____

Day 360

For the time will come when people will not put up with sound doctrine. Instead, to suit their own desires, they will gather around them a great number of teachers to say what their itching ears want to hear. They will turn their ears away from the truth and turn aside to myths. But you, keep your head in all situations, endure hardship, do the work of an evangelist, discharge all the duties of your ministry. 2 Timothy 4:3-5

We can see Paul's warning being evident in our present world, men following doctrines which gratify their desires. Examples are seen in the moral decline of many christian leaders, competitiveness in ministry, distrust of leadership, conspiracy theories and world religions such as Buddism, Hinduism, Taoism, Scientology, Mormonism, Jehovahs Witness, and more. See Psalm 32:8 and learn it.

Prayer: Dear Heavenly Father, help me to keep my mind on you, to keep me strong in my trust and faith in you. I choose to hear your voice and lean into you.

Journal

___

___

___

___

___

Day 361

For I am already being poured out like a drink offering, and the time for my departure is near. I have fought the good fight, I have finished the race, I have kept the faith. Now there is in store for me the crown of righteousness, which the Lord, the righteous Judge, will award to me on that day - and not only to me, but also to all who have longed for his appearing. 2 Timothy 4:6-8

Paul is aware of his impending death. He was beheaded, becoming a martyr, on the Apian Way during Nero's reign. Here he looks back over his life's work and looks forward to his everlasting life with Jesus.

Prayer: Dear Heavenly Father, thank you that I can hope in you, for you are my shield and song. In you my heart rejoices, no matter what the world hurls at me, I rest in you. Amen.

Journal

____

____

____

____

____

Day 362

Do your best to come to me quickly, for Demas, because he loved this world, has deserted me and has gone to Thessalonica. Crescens has gone to Galatia, and Titus to Dalmatia. Only Luke is with me. Get Mark and bring him with you, because he is helpful to me in my ministry. I sent Tychicus to Ephesus. When you come, bring the cloak that I left with Carpus at Troas, and my scrolls, especially the parchments. 2 Timothy 4:9-13

In this passage, we can feel Paul's humanness - his loneliness, his need for his friends, for warmth and comfort, for mental stimulation, and for Christian fellowship.

Prayer: Dear Heavenly Father, thank you for comfort you bring to us through other christian men and women. Thank you also, that you encamp around us and you deliver us from all our fears. Amen.

Journal

____

____

____

____

____

Day 363

Alexander the metalworker did me a great deal of harm. The Lord will repay him for what he has done. You too should be on your guard against him, because he strongly opposed our message. At my first defense, no one came to my support, but everyone deserted me. May it not be held against them. But the Lord stood at my side and gave me strength, so that through me the message might be fully proclaimed and all the Gentiles might hear it. And I was delivered out of the lion's mouth. 2 Timothy 4:14-17

Have you ever experienced, or are you experiencing persecution? Think on Paul's words in verse 17 - But the Lord stood by my side and gave me strength.' Take hold of the hand of Jesus and rest in him during those times.

Prayer: Dear Heavenly Father, thank you for your promises to rescue me. I choose to take refuge in you. You are close to me and save me deliver me from my troubles. Amen.

Journal

____

____

____

____

____

Day 364

The Lord will rescue me from every evil attack and will bring me safely to his heavenly kingdom. To him be glory for ever and ever. Amen. Greet Priscilla and Aquila and the household of Onesiphorus. Erastus stayed in Corinth, and I left Trophies sick in Miletus. Do your best to get here before winter. Eubulus greets you, and so do Pudens, Linus, Claudia and all the brothers and sisters. The Lord be with your spirit. Grace be with you all. 2 Timothy 4:18-22

Memorize verse 18, 'The Lord will rescue me from every evil attack and will bring me safely to his heavenly kingdom.' and use it when the enemy attacks you. This is your sword of the Spirit. Keep your stand and continue with the wonderful promises of Jesus in your heart. Amen.

Prayer: Dear Heavenly Father, thank you that you are not far from me. I take delight in you and trust you. Amen.

Journal

____

____

____

____

____

Day 365

Paul, a servant of God and an apostle of Jesus Christ to further the faith of God's elect and their knowledge of the truth that leads to godliness - in the hope of eternal life, which God, who does not lie, promised before the beginning of time, and which not at his appointed season he has brought to light through the preaching entrusted to me by the command of God our Savior, To Titus, my true son in our common faith: Grace and peace from God the Father and Christ Jesus our Savior. Titus 1:1-4

Paul writes this letter to his colleague in the ministry of Jesus Christ, Titus, who is ministering on the island of Crete. The fledgling church was in danger of the heresy from Judaisers . Paul wrote this letter to encourage him and to instruct him on matters such as leading the church and refuting the false teaching.

Prayer: Dear Heavenly Father, thank you for men and women in my life *(name them)* who come beside me to encourage me in my faith. Amen.

Journal

____

____

____

____

Day 366

The reason I left you in Crete was that you might put in order what was left unfinished and appoint elders in every town, as I directed you. An elder must be blameless, faithful to his wife, a man whose children believe and are not open to the charge of being wild and disobedient. Since an overseer manages God's household, he must be blameless - not overbearing, not quick-tempered, not given to drunkenness, not violent, not pursuing dishonest gain. Rather, he must be hospitable, one who loves what is good, who is self-controlled, upright, holy and disciplined. He must hold firmly to the trustworthy message as it has been taught, so that he can encourage others by sound doctrine and refute those who oppose it. Titus 1:5-9

We see the list of expected characteristics of elders and overseers, as we saw in Timothy's letter. Paul is explaining these same things to Titus, in order for the church to be managed by trustworthy, faithful men who follow the Lord Jesus with all their heart, and with their lives. They are an example to those within the church as well as those outside the church looking in.

How does your example show within the church and to those who are outside the church looking in? Journal your thoughts.

Prayer: Dear Heavenly Father, make my steps firm, though I stumble you will uphold me with your hand. Keep me true to you as I walk with my hand in yours each day. Amen.

Journal

____

____

____

____

____

Day 367

For there are many rebellious people, full of meaningless talk and deception, especially those of the circumcision group. They must be silenced, because they are disrupting whole households by teaching things they ought not to teach - and that for the sake of dishonest gain. One of Crete's own prophets has said it: 'Cretans are always liars, evil brutes, lazy gluttons.' This saying is true. Therefore, rebuke them sharply, so that they will be sound in the faith and will pay no attention to Jewish myths or to the merely human commands of those who reject the truth. To the pure, all things are pure, but to those who are corrupted and do not believe, nothing is pure. In fact, both their minds and consciences are corrupted. They claim to know God, but by their actions they deny him. They are detestable, disobedient and unfit for doing anything good. Titus 1:10-16

Now we see Paul refuting the Judaisers. He called them the 'circumcision group'. For a review as to how the Apostles managed the Judiasers heresy, see Acts 15:23-31

Prayer: Dear Heavenly Father, create in me a pure heart, and renew a steadfast spirit within me. My sacrifice to you, O God, is a broken spirit and a broken, contrite heart. Ps 51:10,17. Amen.

Journal

____

____

____

____

____

Day 368

You, however, must teach what is appropriate to sound doctrine. Teach the older men to be temperate, worthy of respect, self-controlled, and sound in faith, in love and in endurance. Likewise, teach the older women to be reverent in the way they live, not to be slanderers or addicted to much wine, but to teach what is good. Then they can urge the younger women to love their husbands and children, to be self-controlled and pure, to be busy at home, to be kind, and to be subject to their husbands, so that no one will malign the word of God. Titus 2:1-5

Titus 2 contains sage advise to men and women in the management of their lives. Men to be temperate, worthy of respect, self-controlled, sound in faith, love and endurance. Women to be reverent, to teach what is good, to mentor younger women in their faith, and to be subject to their husbands. By doing these things, the Lord will be honored.

Do you mentor another person who is younger than you in your faith? Are you being mentored by someone who cares about you? Think and pray about mentoring someone in their faith, to help them to grow to become more like Jesus. Journal your thoughts.

Prayer: Dear Heavenly Father, place someone on my heart that I may reach out to them to mentor them in the christian faith. Amen.

Journal

____

____

____

____

____

Day 369

Similarly, encourage the young men to be self-controlled. In everything set them an example by doing what is good. In your teaching show integrity, seriousness and soundness of speech that cannot be condemned, so that those who oppose you may be ashamed because they have nothing bad to say about us. Teach slaves to be subject to their masters in everything, to try to please them, not to talk back to them, and not to steal from them, but to show that they can be fully trusted, so that in every way they will make the teaching about God our Savior attractive. Titus 2:6-10

Are you impressed with the advise Paul is sharing with Titus. May we also take the words into our being and show integrity, seriousness in our belief as we live for the Lord, and soundness of speech as we share the gospel to those around us. By being transparent and honest, people will see Jesus living through us.

Prayer: Dear Heavenly Father, I trust you to instruct and teach me your ways so that I may follow the path you show me day by day. Amen.

Journal

____
____
____
____
____

Day 370

For the grace of God has appeared that offers salvation to all people. It teaches us to say 'No' to ungodliness and worldly passions, and to live self-controlled, upright and godly lives in this present age, while we wait for the blessed hope - the appearing of the glory of our great God and Savior, Jesus Christ, who gave himself for us to redeem us from all wickedness and to purify for himself a people that are his very own, eager to do what is good. These, then, are the things you should teach. Encourage and rebuke with all authority. Do not let anyone despise you. Titus 2:11-15

God's grace not only saves us, but also teaches us. It teaches us how to live for him and what to throw away from our old life. The blood of Jesus Christ which was shed on the cross for our redemption, covers our sins from God's eyes, and in his sight we are acceptable to him. Because Jesus Christ died and rose from the dead, proving he is God (Godhead includes Father, Son and Holy Spirit), we are freed, by his power, from the curse of sin and wickedness, and cleansed from our old life. In Him, we walk as purified people belonging to Him.

Prayer: Dear Heavenly Father, You are incredibly amazing, and I humbly adore you. There are no words for me to speak my heart of love to you. Instead I say 'Hallelujah and amen.' Amen.

Journal

____

____

____

____

____

Day 371

Remind the people to be subject to rulers and authorities, to be obedient, to be ready to do whatever is good, to slander no one, to be peaceable and considerate, and always to be gentle toward everyone. At one time we too were foolish, disobedient, deceived and enslaved by all kinds of passions and pleasures. We lived in malice and envy, being hated and hating one another. But when the kindness and love of God our Savior appeared, he saved us, not because of righteous things we had done, but because of his mercy. He saved us through the washing of rebirth and renewal by the Holy Spirit, whom he poured out on us generously through Jesus Christ our Savior, so that, having been justified by his grace, we might become heirs having the hope of eternal life. Titus 3:1-7

God our Savior saved us because of his mercy. Then he generously poured on us the Holy Spirit, through Jesus Christ. He has given us the best 'ever' free gift anyone would ever want. The free gift of becoming one with him, through the redemptive work of Jesus Christ on the cross and through his resurrection. The Holy Spirit was poured on humans fifty days after Jesus Christ's ascension to Heaven, and he remains with us today, loving on us, caring for us, guiding us, prompting us, giving us words to speak in season, and ever so much more. Journal the ways you see the Holy Spirit working in your life.

Prayer: Dear Heavenly Father, I adore you, lay my life before you, how I love you. Amen.

Journal

Day 372

This is a trustworthy saying. And I want you to stress these things, so that those who have trusted in God may be careful to devote themselves to doing what is good. These things are excellent and profitable for everyone. But avoid foolish controversies and genealogies and arguments and quarrels about the law, because these are unprofitable and useless. Warn a divisive person once and then warn them a second time. After that, have nothing to do with them. You may be sure that such people are warped and sinful; they are self-condemned. Titus 3:8-11

We all are aware that controversies are useless, timewasters, emotional and detrimental. Paul advises us to stay away from them. His advise is to warn the divisive person two times, then have nothing more to do with them. Sound advise. How do you manage these people in your life? Journal your thoughts.

Prayer: Dear Heavenly Father, Keep me from getting involved with controversies and divisive people. Keep my focus on you. Give me the words in season to speak at those times when emotions are high. Thank you for your promise to never leave me. Amen.

Journal

____

____

____

____

____

Day 373

As soon as I send Artemis or Tychicus to you, do your best to come to me at Nicololis, because I have decided to winter there. Do everything you can to help Zenas the lawyer and Apollos on their way and see that they have everything they need. Our people must learn to devote themselves to doing what is good, in order to provide for urgent needs and not live unproductive lives. Everyone with me sends you greetings. Greet those who love us in the faith. Grace be with you all. Titus 3:12-15

I love Paul's endings. He always includes common friend's names, as well as others who are interested and involved in the Lord's work. He also concludes with pronouncing God's grace on everyone. May God's grace be on you as well.

Prayer: Dear Heavenly Father, Thank you for friends, those whom are in my life who know you as well as those in my life who do not know you. May your grace be upon them all. Amen.

Journal

Day 374

Paul, a prisoner of Christ Jesus, and Timothy our brother, To Philemon our dear friend and fellow worker - also to Appia our sister and Archippus our fellow soldier - and the church that meets in your home. Grace and peace to you from God our Father and the Lord Jesus Christ. I always thank my God as I remember you in my prayers, because I hear about your love for all his holy people and your faith in the Lord Jesus. I pray that your partnership with us in the faith may be effective in deepening your understanding of every good thing we share for the sake of Christ. Your love has given me great joy and encouragement, because you, brother, have refreshed the hearts of the Lord's people. Philemon 1-7

Paul and Timothy write this letter to Philemon, and the members of the church at Colossae. It is a letter to ask Philemon to show grace and compassion to his runaway slave, Onesimus, who became a christian and is now returning to Philemon. With Philemon being a christian master and Onesimus being a christian slave, they are now christian brothers. Paul begins his letter with his introduction, and to whom the letter is addressed. He always says positive things at the outset of his letters, and this time he thanks God because of their love and faith in the Lord Jesus and the joy and encouragement they have been to him.

Prayer: Dear Heavenly Father, thank you for the example we see with Philemon and Onesimus, being christian brothers, yet the social scale is opposing for each of them. Thank you that your love does not show any boundaries or biases. You came to save the whole world, which means the rich, the poor and everyone in between. Amen.

Journal

____

____

____

____

____

Day 375

Therefore, although in Christ I could be bold and order you to do what you ought to do, yet I prefer to appeal to you on the basis of love. It is as none other than Paul - an old man and now also a prisoner of Christ Jesus - that I appeal to you for my son Onesimus, who became my son while I was in chains. Formerly he was useless to you, but now he has become useful both to you and to me. Philemon 8-11

Now we see Paul approaching the subject of asking Philemon to be compassionate and merciful to Onesimus. Paul is not telling him what to do, but instead is suggesting the that Onesimus is useful to both Philemon and Paul - probably in the furtherance of the Kingdom of God. By his own volition Philemon will forgive him and accept him back into his household. Forgiveness is an integral part of living for Jesus Christ - he forgave us from our debt of sin. The Lord's prayer tells us to pray, 'Forgive us our debts as we have forgiven our debtors.' Matthew 6:12.

Today, think about those people and situations you need to forgive.

Prayer: Dear Heavenly Father, I choose to forgive *(name the people)* for *(name the infringement)*. I want to clear make right that broken relationship between them and me, so you will forgive me the same way I forgive others. I am indebted to you for your forgiveness to me. Amen.

Journal

____

____

____

____

Day 376

I am sending him - who is my very heart - back to you. I would have liked to keep him with me so that he could take your place in helping me while I am in chains for the gospel. But I did not want to do anything without your consent, so that any favor you do would not seem forced but would be voluntary. Perhaps the reason he was separated from you for a little while was that you might have him back forever - no longer as a slave, but better than a slave, as a dear brother. He is very dear to me but even dearer to you, both as a fellow man and as a brother in the Lord. Philemon 12-16

Can you sense the love Paul has for both Philemon and Onesimus. He is encouraging both men to do the honorable thing - Philemon to forgive Onesimus, and Onesimus to return to Philemon, his master - both being very hard in their cultural context. But, because of our Lord Jesus, love wins through.

Have you had some hard decisions to make? How did you manage them? Journal your thoughts.

Prayer: Dear Heavenly Father, thank you that you are always with me, when things are going well, as well as when things are going down the drain. Thank you I can reach out to you and put my hand in yours when I need support, encouragement, especially when life is hard. Amen.

Journal

____

____

____

____

____

Day 377

So, if you consider me a partner, welcome him as you would welcome me. If he has done you any wrong or owes you anything, charge it to me. I, Paul, am writing this with my own hand. I will pay it back - not to mention that you owe me your very self. I do wish, brother, that I may have some benefit from you in the Lord; refresh my heart in Christ. Confident of your obedience, I write to you, knowing that you will do even more than I ask. And one thing more: Prepare a guest room for me, because I have to be restored to you in answer to your prayers. Epaphras, my fellow prisoner in Christ Jesus, sends you greetings. And so do Mark, Aristarchus, Demas and Luke, my fellow workers. The grace of the Lord Jesus Christ be with your spirit. Philemon 17-25

Verse 17 is the climax of the letter, and Paul puts himself in the place of Onesimus, stating that he, Paul, will pay back anything Onesimus owes Philemon.

Paul's letter to Philemon helps us to see those who may otherwise fall through the cracks in our society, with no assistance from anyone or any organization. We may not be able to undo injustices, but we can have compassion and reach out to those in need.

Prayer: Dear Heavenly Father, let me be a vessel for you to use to help those around me who have been forgotten. May I show them your love and compassion be caring for them and giving them hope through you. Amen.

Journal

____

____

____

____

____

Dear friend,

Thank you for staying with me as we have drawn from the Holy Bible with scripture and reflections/inspiration together for the last 376 days. We have completed Paul's letters from the New Testament, through this book as well as day to day Reflections: Acts, Corinthians, Romans. I trust your heart has been opened to see the relevance of God's word in our society, and in your life. I trust you have been encouraged to assimilate God's word into your heart. Psalm 119,105: 'Your word is a lamp to my feet and a light to my path.'

Continue with me as we embark on exploring God's word again through Day-to-Day Reflections: Hebrews, James, Peter, John, Jude, Revelation.

'The Lord bless you and keep you, The Lord make his face shine upon you and be gracious to you. The Lord turn his face toward you and give you peace.' Numbers 6:24-26

Blessings,

Beverley